# SHALOM/SALAAM: A Resource for Jewish-Muslim Dialogue

Gary M. Bretton-Granatoor

Andrea L. Weiss

UAHC Press

# ACKNOWLEDGEMENTS

The publication of *Shalom / Salaam: A Resource for Jewish-Muslim Dialogue* would not have been possible without the insight and assistance of many individuals.

We thank those who contributed original articles to this project: Abdelwahab Hechiche, Professor in the Department of Government and International Affairs at the University of Southern Florida; Leonard A. Kravitz, Professor of Midrash and Homiletics at the Hebrew Union College-Jewish Institute of Religion in New York; J. Dudley Woodberry, Dean and Associate Professor of Islamic Studies at the School of World Mission at the Fuller Theological Seminary.

We are grateful to Jonathan Sarna, Chairperson of Near Eastern and Judaic Studies at Brandeis University, and the Susan and David Wilstein Institute of Jewish Policy Studies for permission to reprint Dr. Sarna's article. The article originally appeared in *Jewish Identity in America*, edited by David M. Gordis and Yoav Ben-Horin (Los Angeles: University of Judaism, 1991). The article by Reuven Firestone, Professor of Medieval Jewish History at the Hebrew Union College-Jewish Institute of Religion in Los Angeles, was published in the *CCAR Journal* (Spring 1992). We thank Dr. Firestone and Rabbi Lawrence Englander, Editor of the *CCAR Journal*, for allowing us to reprint the article.

Many others contributed to *Shalom / Salaam* by sharing their knowledge and opinions about Jewish-Muslim dialogue over the telephone or in personal meetings: Dr. Gutbi Ahmed, Imam Dr. M. Salem Agwa, Dr. Mahmoud Ayoub, Dr. Eugene Borowitz, Rabbi Jayr Davis, Dr. Yvonne Yazbeck Haddad, Rabbi Martin Lawson, Sister Glady Muhammad, Dr. Azim Nanji, Ms. Sunni Rumsey-Ahmed, Dr. Muzammil Siddiqui, Dr. Michael Signer, Ms. Karen Wood. We also appreciate the efforts of Dr. Philip Miller and Dr. Mian Ashraf, who read drafts of the programs.

In addition, we would like to thank the UAHC Department of Production (especially Pat Vallone, Vivian Fernandez, Helayne Friedland) and the UAHC Department of Publications (Stu Benick and Sharyn Aviv). Above all, we are indebted to the tireless efforts of Maud Prince, who typed and helped edit many of the manuscripts.

Rabbi Jerome Davidson deserves special recognition for his ongoing support and guidance as Chair of the UAHC Committee on Interreligious Affairs. He and his congregation, Temple Beth El of Great Neck, have already demonstrated the fruits that Jewish-Muslim dialogue can yield.

**Rabbi Gary M. Bretton-Granatoor**
*Director, UAHC Dept. of Interreligious Affairs*
*Associate Director, Commission on*
*Social Action of Reform Judaism*

**Rabbi Andrea L. Weiss**
*UAHC Dept. of Interreligious Affairs*

# TABLE OF CONTENTS

# PREFACE

## A. Goals

*Shalom / Salaam: A Resource for Jewish-Muslim Dialogue* approaches Jewish-Muslim relations from two directions: education and participation. The articles provide an introduction to Jewish-Muslim dialogue and background on Jewish-Muslim relations. The programs further the study of Judaism and Islam through dialogue and interaction.

The first four articles help lay the groundwork for dialogue by addressing the questions: Why should we engage in Jewish-Muslim dialogue? How can we best do so? The remaining pieces place Jewish-Muslim dialogue within a historical context, presenting Muslim and Jewish perspectives on the past links between Judaism and Islam.

The programs are designed to meet several basic goals: to teach the participants about Islam and Judaism and to establish relationships on personal and communal levels. The format and content of the programs work toward achieving these aims by providing numerous opportunities for the participants to teach each other about their religious traditions and to share with one another the struggles and celebrations of their religious lives.

As the titles of the first and last programs indicate, this eight-session dialogue is seen as the start of a journey. To make the path of Jewish-Muslim dialogue a meaningful one, each program attempts to foster respect, trust, and friendship and to elicit greater understanding and sensitivity as to what it means to be an American Muslim or an American Jew.

# B. Getting Started

The first step in establishing a dialogue is an obvious one: bringing together a group of interested Muslims and Jews. In addition to contacting the appropriate religious institutions in your area, the following organizations, among others, will be able to provide assistance and resources:

UAHC Office of Interreligious Affairs
Rabbi Gary Bretton-Granatoor, Director
838 Fifth Avenue, New York, NY 10021
(212) 249-0100 (ext. 485)

The Muslim World League
Dr. Dawud Assad
President, Council of Mosques of the U.S.A.
134 West 26th Street, New York, NY 10001
(212) 627-4033

In creating this resource guide, we have attempted to make running the dialogue as easy as possible. One need not be a Jewish or Muslim scholar in order to facilitate the programs, nor is a great deal of outside research required. Instead, the programs can be run by a Jewish and a Muslim facilitator with modest preparation.

Before the first session, the facilitators should set the meeting dates and prepare a schedule listing the date, topic, and location of each session (for distribution at the first meeting). If possible, the meeting site should alternate between the synagogue and the mosque.

Also in advance of the first program, the participants should receive a copy of *Shalom/Salaam* and read the four introductory articles ("The Need for Jewish-Muslim Dialogue" by Gary Bretton-Granatoor, "From Disease to Dialogue" by Andrea Weiss, "Lessons from Christian-Muslim Dialogue for Jewish-Muslim Dialogue" by J. Dudley Woodberry, and "Religious Identity in the Changing World of American Religion" by Jonathan Sarna). These articles will help prepare the participants for dialogue (the remaining articles are incorporated into later programs).

In preparation for the second program, the video *Abraham and His Children* should be ordered from the Jewish Chautauqua Society: 838 Fifth Avenue, New York, NY 10021, (212) 570-0707.

# THE NEED FOR JEWISH-MUSLIM DIALOGUE

## Gary M. Bretton-Granatoor

For far too long the Jewish community has allowed itself to live with misconceptions and misinformation about the Muslim community. After all, newspaper headlines and contemporary politics have overshadowed a 1,300 year relationship, making it easy for us to forget about a shared history with long-standing and positive roots.

Just as Judaism has had a powerful impact on the Muslim community and culture, Islam has had a tremendous influence on our own people and past. Where would we be today were it not for the emphasis on science and mathematics, so central to Islamic thought, which nourished great Jewish thinkers like Saadia Gaon, Yehuda HaLevi and Maimonides? Islamic debates on faith and good deeds made by the Mutazila found their way into Maimonides' *Guide of the Perplexed*. Medieval Jewish philosophers such as Saadia HaGaon and Yehuda HaLevi were similarly shaped by their Islamic world. In fact, we would not have been introduced to the great Hellenistic thinkers such as Plato or Aristotle were it not for Islamic translations of these works by such Muslim scholars as al-Farabi and Averroes, which were read by these and other Jewish thinkers.

To a large extent, a lack of knowledge has colored our relationship with the Muslim community over the past century. For example, although we often hear the words Muslim and Arab used interchangeably, it is important to note that only twenty percent of the world's Muslims are Arab. Indeed, how much do we Jews truly know about the Islamic world? We hear words like *Jihad* and *Ramadan*, but do we know what they really mean? How much do politics of the Middle East intrude upon a relationship that can potentially prove fruitful and powerful? These are the misconceptions we must begin to dispel today. It is this lack of knowledge that we must counter with education and dialogue. Here, today, we must remove the political agenda which stands as a road-block on the path of a renewed relationship with our Muslim brothers and sisters. We must commit ourselves to walking down this path together, for are we not all children of one father, Abraham, and children of One God?

In the beginning of our relationship, Jews and Christians held a place of special importance in the Muslim world. We were People of the Book and exempted from efforts at conversion. In certain places where Islamic rule held sway, Jews were employed in higher government positions. The Qur'an, the holy text of the Islamic world, made use of Jewish and Christian legal and cultic principles as a basis upon which their own practices evolved.

Certain basic principles of the faith of Islam find consonance within the Jewish world. The dialectic of the written word with the oral tradition—which we in the Jewish tradition refer to as Torah, the written law, and Mishnah and Talmud, the oral tradition—finds parallels in Islamic tradition. The Qur'an is the written law, but it cannot be studied alone in order to discover the principles of Islam. Their oral tradition, stories and commentaries much like our *midrashim* and *meforshim*, are found in the *Hadith* and the *Qisas al-Anbiya* (Legends of the Prophets—whose title sounds like Pirke Avot, our Legends of the Fathers).

The heart of Islam is found in the Qur'an, which contains the Ten Commandments, the Six Articles of Belief, and the Five Pillars of Faith. Surely, the Ten Commandments are familiar to most readers. The Five Pillars of Faith are: 1) recital of the creed; 2) prayer five times a day, facing Mecca; 3) giving tithes to support the poor and expand the faith; 4) observation of the fast of Ramadan which commemorates the revelation of the Qur'an (much like our Shavuot); and 5) a pilgrimage to

Mecca if physically and financially able. The Six Articles of Belief are: 1) God is One; 2) the Qur'an is God's inspired book; 3) God's angels are heavenly beings created to serve God and they oppose evil spirits; 4) God sent prophets to earth at stated times for stated purposes and makes no distinction between them (the last of which was Mohammed—others include Noah, Abraham, Moses, David and many of the Hebrew Prophets); 5) the Day of Judgement will find good and evil weighed in the balance; 6) the lives and acts of people are known to God, yet people are the architects of their own destiny, free to make or mar their own future through lives of honest endeavor.

Over time, disputes arose between the followers of Islam and their Jewish and Christian neighbors. While there is a substantial corpus of polemical writings against the Christians, there were fewer polemics against Jews, though they are not entirely absent from our collective past. There were Islamic leaders who leaned favorably towards Jews and Judaism, though it has been assumed that the number of Christian converts to Islam caused a sharp rise in anti-Jewish sentiment and writings. It is interesting to note that the polemics against Jews and Judaism from the Muslim world follow the same approach as Christian polemical writings. The charge levied against the Jews was that after each new faith emerged, Jews held fast to their own faith and refused to follow the new path that each religion taught. And yet, one cannot escape the fact that a large number of Jewish teachings appear in both the Qur'an and *Hadith* literature. Conversely, the influence of *fiqh* (Islamic jurisprudence) is felt palpably in geonic *halacha* (rabbinic law), especially in matters of inheritance, gifts, oaths, usury and loans.

Our past history is filled with confluences and dissonances, positive interchange and negative interaction. Yet Jews today focus primarily on recent events, not on this rich, complex past. The pejorative and negative stereotypes promulgated by the press cast a dark shadow on a noble people, its history, and its faith. We Jews have accepted these unfortunate images and used them to widen the rift that exists between our peoples. It is that chasm that we hope to narrow by opening the road to true dialogue and interchange.

Our first step is the simplest—we must open our doors and extend our hands and greet our Muslim brothers and sisters. We must then learn about the Muslim world and the Islamic faith and introduce them to the richness of our own tradition. That means learning about their holidays, their calendar, their primary teachings, and their religious aspirations and sharing how we practice our faith, our holidays, our calendar, our traditions. As we examine our similarities and appreciate our differences, we will find our common concerns and learn what hurts each other. Only then, after all these tasks have moved us significantly along the path, can we introduce politics into the dialogue. Without the prerequisite understanding of each tradition, the discussion of politics can only devolve into rhetoric and demagoguery.

It is with the hope in mind, that *Shalom / Salaam: A Resource for Jewish-Muslim Dialogue* will be used to bring about face to face dialogue between American Muslims and American Jews. We pray that this new undertaking will bring us closer to our Muslim brothers and sisters and thus bring about a more peaceful and harmonious world—the world that the One God ordained for us.

# FROM DISEASE TO DIALOGUE:

## AN INTRODUCTION TO JEWISH-MUSLIM DIALOGUE

## Andrea L. Weiss

The book of Leviticus describes the following scene: A man returns home at the end of the day, expecting to find his house exactly as he left it that morning. But much to his surprise, when he opens the door, he immediately discovers that his house has undergone a bizarre transformation: a thick, musty smell fills the air, patches of red and brown mar the walls, and the plaster is cracked and crumbling to the ground. Startled by these changes, the owner of the house turns around and runs outside. Rushing toward the priest, he cries: "Something like a plague has appeared on my house!" (Lev. 14:35).

The priest immediately orders all objects removed from the house—lest anything become unclean. He then approaches, opens the door, and surveys the walls. His fingertips brush the stones—cold, damp, and moldy. He looks around. "What type of house is this?" he wonders. "What has caused such damage to its walls?"

On one level, the house I speak of is simply a stone structure which stood at one time in the land of Canaan, a house inhabited by an Israelite long ago. But on another level, the level of metaphor, this scene presents an image of the prevailing attitude toward dialogue between Muslims and Jews.

Most likely, this probably was not your first association. After all, what does a house infected with a strange, plague-like substance possibly have to do with Jewish-Muslim dialogue? Strange as it may seem, however, the image of the diseased house is useful for those interested in Jewish-Muslim dialogue, for it helps us understand what we need to overcome in order to establish a positive relationship and what is at stake in our ability to do so.

The empty house of stone and plaster represents our potential to build meaningful relationships with our Muslim neighbors—the chance, as individuals and as a community, to share our stories and teach each other who we really are. Located in Detroit or Minneapolis, New York or Vero Beach, at a meeting of local clergy, a college Hillel, or an exchange between a synagogue and a mosque—in a sense, this house exists wherever Jews and Muslims live, work, and play side-by-side. Wherever we transform a coincidence of coexistence into an opportunity for education and friendship, that is where we find the house. That is where Jewish-Muslim dialogue can begin.

But many people think it won't work. "Don't even try," they say. "Stay out of the house." "Something like a plague has appeared on its walls."

Within this metaphoric house of Jewish-Muslim dialogue, the plague-like substance that covers the walls consists of the obstacles which threaten to interrupt the dialogue or prevent the conversation from even beginning. The list of potential obstacles is a long one: politics, theology, history, fear of the other and the unknown. Many are the sources of possible confrontation or ruin.

First, the plague of world politics: According to Dr. Azim Nanji of the University of Florida, the regional issues of the Middle East have become globalized. As a result, Jews and Muslims outside the Middle East meet one another with "a political cloud hanging over their heads" which threatens to overshadow all other aspects of the relationship. [1] Even though Arabs make up only twenty percent of the Islamic population, this grey, ominous political cloud obscures our vision and leads many to believe that the Middle East is all we have to talk about or that Jewish-Muslim dialogue and the Arab-Israeli conflict are one and the same. Almost unanimously, those who have attempted to build bridges between American Muslims and Jews agree that dialogue cannot begin with world politics. If our efforts are to be successful, we must first focus our attention on the West, not on the Middle East.

Next, the plague of misunderstanding: Some think Muslims are all terrorists or fundamentalists. Others believe Islam is archaic and unchanging. "They won't talk to us." "They can't understand us." "They simply don't care." Stereotypes, ignorance, fear—something like a plague has appeared on the wall.

"Lock the door."
"Bar the windows."
"Abandon the house."

Such was the message I received when I started working on *Shalom / Salaam: A Resource for Jewish-Muslim Dialogue*. Knowing very little about Islam and never having spoken at length with a Muslim, my research began by talking to Muslim and Jewish scholars and religious leaders and by hoarding all the books I could find with the words "Islam" or "Muslim" in the title.

And that's how I learned about the plague. That's when I discovered that while many books have been published on Jews and Muslims in seventh century Arabia or in medieval Egypt or Spain, almost nothing has been written on the contemporary relationship between Muslims and Jews. In contrast to the significant amount of time and energy invested in participating in and reflecting on Jewish-Christian dialogue, interaction between Muslims and Jews has, so far, been relatively rare. Shrouded in pessimism and mistrust, Jewish-Muslim dialogue has long been avoided or ignored.

This discovery leads to a question that must be asked, and answered, in order for meaningful dialogue to take place. And that is: Why begin now? Amidst the silence, the hesitation, and the many challenges, why even begin such a long and arduous process? Facing crumbling stones and decaying plaster, why even try repairing the house?

Answering these questions requires us to look closely and honestly at who we are. First, we must recognize that as Americans, we live with certain myths about ourselves. Even in this age of multi-culturalism, lawmakers and community leaders speak of the Judeo-Christian values that guide our country; and politicians and clergy herald the United States as a tripartite nation—a society comprised of Protestants, Catholics, and Jews. We slice Mom's homemade apple pie into three equal pieces, pretending all three religions share nearly equal influence and representation, assuming we are the only faith traditions that make up the pie.

But in fact, as compared to approximately eighty million Protestants, fifty-five million Roman Catholics, and six million Jews, there are now four and a half million Muslims in the United States. The number of mosques and Islamic centers in this country has quadrupled in the past ten years, and by the year 2015, only twenty-two years from now, experts estimate that Muslims will outnumber Jews and demonstrate an increasingly larger influence on American thought. Islam, now the second largest religion in the world, will soon become the second largest religion in the United States.

Arithmetic alone mandates that we reconsider how we slice the pie. Statistics call upon us to question how our priorities and our identity will change in this newly configured world. What will it mean for us if we no longer see ourselves as an isolated minority within a pervasively Christian society, but instead as one of many smaller segments of American religious life? Politically and psychologically, as the image of our predominantly Judeo-Christian nation fades away, will Jews experience a decline in status or an increased sense of belonging and power?

Population surveys and demographic predictions force us to ask difficult questions and confront the fear and vulnerability that often accompany change. But they also remind us that as a religious minority in America, we are not alone. In 1993, not in 2015, we must explore what the growth of Islam in means for us as Jews. Today, not twenty-two years from now, we must begin a journey of dialogue and support.

While demographics may motivate us to reach out to the Islamic community, mathematics can exert only limited might. Statistics cannot remove a plague from the walls of a house; numbers cannot build bridges, alter stereotypes, or teach a Jew what it means to be a Muslim and a Muslim what it means to be a Jew.

At its best, interreligious dialogue is an "enrichment to life" [2] and an opportunity for "self-transformation and self-transcendence." [3] To reach these goals, however, partners in dialogue must come together, not because of the threat of demographics, but because of the importance of education and understanding, the benefits of communication and connectedness, and the promise of where the relationship can lead.

Most importantly, we should commit ourselves to engaging in dialogue, not merely for all we have to gain, but for who we are. We are Americans living in a pluralistic society; pluralism demands interaction and cooperation. We are Jews are taught of righteousness and compassion, Jews who learn: "When a stranger resides with you in your land, you shall not wrong him. The stranger who resides with you shall be to you as one of your citizens; you shall love him as yourself, for you were strangers in the land of Egypt" (Lev. 19:33-4).

As American Muslims and American Jews, we have all been strangers: A third-generation Jew in Boston with Polish roots, a Muslim whose grandparents moved from Lebanon to Detroit, an Israeli-born New Yorker, and an African-American convert to Islam. A Jew in L.A. who grew up speaking Farsi at home, an engineer from Pakistan, and the daughter of Egyptian parents who sits on the board of her local mosque.

We all wander. We have all been strangers. Surely we can speak to one another face to face, as one speaks to a friend. Surely we can find a place of meeting where, together, we can replace assumptions and generalizations with names and faces, ignorance with insight, and fear and hostility with friendship and hope.

When American Jews and American Muslims meet, we do so as men and women who wear many masks. Religion, ethnicity, nationality—in our complex world, we come together as complex individuals and diverse communities. When we enable ourselves to share our stories, we will find the "barricade of otherness" [4] begin to break down. In their words, we can hear echoes of our past experiences and present struggles. In our words, they can find a point of reference and support. Strangers can become allies; the alienated can find themselves less powerless and less alone.

Looking for a way to listen to contemporary Muslim voices, I discovered a book entitled *Islamic Values in the United States*. An in-depth sociological study of three Islamic communities, the book explores many facets of what it means to be a practicing Muslim in the United States. The analysis of extensive interviews and surveys portrays a community confronting the key question of how to live an Islamic life in a non-Muslim country. To what degree is one able to, or interested in, becoming socially integrated into American culture? Especially for the large numbers of first generation American Muslims, how does one deal with the dual, but not mutually reinforcing, relationship between an allegiance to Islam and a responsibility to one's newly adopted country? [5]

Attempting to answer these questions, the book tells many stories. Here are just a few:

A group of Muslims from one country established a mosque in their community. Following a later influx of new immigrants from another country, however, the population and practices of the mosque began to change. With the new immigrants the dominant force in the mosque, Arabic became the primary language, social activities were no longer held, and women were restricted to traditional dress and a separate area for prayer.

A founding member of the mosque discussed the ramifications of this takeover:

Ninety-nine percent of those worshiping there now

know and speak Arabic, so there is no need for English to be spoken in that mosque for a successful religious service. But the Muslim community born here, who have little or no knowledge of Arabic, suffers and continues to suffer because of this reversion. Because the parents themselves don't understand and can't speak Arabic, they cannot insist their children do. You cannot say to your child, "You have to go to learn Arabic, and go to the mosque, and hear the imam speak in Arabic." The child will not stand for that. So for those Muslims born here, the mosques must increase the instruction of Islam through the medium of English, or they are always going to have rejection and a lack of interest. [6]

In 1973, a Muslim woman and her husband moved to the U.S. with their young family. Reflecting upon their first encounter with the Christmas season, she recalled:

In our neighborhood, there were no other Muslims. [A year after we moved, my four year old daughter] was playing in other kid's houses and saw Christmas lights and all sorts of things. She asked me why our holiday doesn't have Christmas trees and lights. I tried to make her understand right there, saying, "Now look, they are Christians. They have their religion and they should celebrate it. We have our religion and we have our celebration at their time." From then on and until today, every Eid [Islamic festival], even if sometimes I can't afford it, I buy each of my children a gift. [7]

To hear these voices is, in part, to hear our own. With an energizing spark of connection and comradery, we remind ourselves that we are not alone in the struggle to maintain a religious and ethnic identity amidst a pluralistic, seemingly secular world. In the laboratory of the synagogue or the mosque, the summer camp or the community center, we are all searching for the magic formula that will enable us to preserve cultural traditions, transmit religious values and practices, and protect ourselves from the allure of assimilation.

Although we cannot forget, or ignore, the differences that distinguish American Muslims and Jews, sharing our insights and observations can yield rich rewards. As we teach each other about our religious practices and communal concerns, dialogue will lead us to many paths of potential assistance and support.

Take, for example, a recent *kashrut* coalition: Because many Muslims abstain from pork and eat only ritually slaughtered meat, they often purchase kosher products. As a result, when the Orthodox Jewish community voiced their concern about animal oil found in steel containers used to carry kosher foods, the Islamic Food and Nutrition Council took part in a joint effort to lobby for change. Together with the Union of Orthodox Jewish Congregations, the Star-K Kosher Certification Board, and a group of Seventh Day Adventists, they successfully urged steel companies to remove the residual animal oils.

Beyond dietary issues, the list of shared concerns and potential areas of cooperation will continue to expand as the relationship grows—from prayer in school and the Religious Freedom Restoration Act to issues concerning the family or social justice. The more we know about each other, the better we will be at building bridges and working together for our common good.

Dr. Gutbi Ahmed, the former North American Director of the Muslim World League, emphasized this message by calling for "more cooperation between our two communities to see common concerns addressed for the good of society." [8] Speaking at the 1991 UAHC Biennial, Dr. Ahmed announced that he had came to the convention with a mandate from the Muslim World League to immediately begin dialogue between Muslims and Jews.

When asked what motivates Muslims to engage in dialogue with Jews, Dr. Ahmed replied that as American neighbors, we need better understanding and cooperation. "We need to stand together," he said, "to confront bias and dispel stereotypes of Muslims and Arabs always as the enemy." [9] Many Muslims echo this desire for dialogue so others will see Islam not as a religion of terror, but as a religion of peace. [10] They want their religion truly represented and respected. They want to be accepted as is, not forced to become like the dominant culture. Some Muslims cite a religious mandate for dialogue, pointing to the special status within Islam of Jews and Christians as 'um al-kitab—People of the Book. [11] Others simply note that we live in "an interconnected, global environment." Such an environment demands dialogue. [13]

As American Muslims and American Jews, we all have much at stake in our potential for dialogue. We must see this process as a necessity, not a luxury, an immediate priority, not something we will deal with later or wait for others to do.

As we stand before the house of Jewish-Muslim dialogue, we must remember that according to the book of Leviticus, a house need not be destroyed because of discolored walls or dilapidated masonry. Instead, seven days after the initial inspection, the priest returns to reexamine the house and, if necessary, to repair the walls. If the plague has spread, he orders the removal of the infected stones and the ruined plaster. New stones replace the old, a fresh coating of plaster covers the walls, and eventually, with no further outbreaks, the house becomes healthy and inhabitable once again.

For Muslims and for Jews, the period of waiting has gone on too long. Together, we must return to the house and start repairing its walls.

From foe to friend and strangers to neighbors, from silence to alliance and disease to dialogue—transformation is truly within our grasp.

---

1.    I am grateful to Dr. Azim Nanji of the University of Florida for the insights he shared with me during a February 5, 1992 telephone conversation.

2.    Hans Kung, "Dialogability and Steadfastness: On Two Complementary Virtues," in *Radical Pluralism and Truth: David Tracy and the Hermeneutics of Religion*, eds. Werner G. Jeanrond and Jennifer L. Rike (New York: The Crossroad Publishing Company, 1991), 239.

3.    Michael A. Signer, "*Communitas et Universitas*: From Theory to Practice in Judeo-Christian Studies," in *When Jews and Christians Meet*, ed. Jakob J.

Petuchowski (New York: State University of New York Press), 77.

4.     Nanji.

5.     Yvonne Yazbeck Haddad and Adair T. Lummis, *Islamic Values in the United States* (New York: Oxford University Press, 1987), 67, 155-156.

6.     Haddad and Lummis, *Islamic Values in the United States*, 42.

7.     Haddad and Lummis, *Islamic Values in the United States*, 95.

8.     Gutbi Ahmed, UAHC Biennial Address, November 3, 1991.

9.     Gutbi Ahmed, telephone conversation, February 3, 1992.

10.    Haddad and Lummis, *Islamic Values in the United States*, 158.

11.    Haddad, telephone conversation, February 3, 1992.

12.    Muzammil Siddiqui, Director of the Islamic Society in Orange County, February 5, 1992 telephone conversation.

13.    Nanji.

# LESSONS FROM CHRISTIAN-MUSLIM DIALOGUE FOR JEWISH-MUSLIM DIALOGUE

## J. Dudley Woodberry

After years of good and bad dialogue with Muslims around the world, I shall try to share first what real dialogue is; second, how it is best prepared for; and finally, some guidelines that have been helpful.

## What Dialogue Is

Dialogue involves two individuals or groups empathetically listening to each other with respect and frankly witnessing to their own faith. I have been in a number of Muslim-Christian "dialogues" on university campuses which at times were more like debates because of lack of empathetic listening.

The attitude required first involves humility. One time an African-American Christian who lives and works with the homeless in Los Angeles and I felt led to apologize to the Imam of the Islamic Center in Orange County for the suffering we Christians had caused Muslims throughout history by such means as the Crusades and colonialism. The results were gratifying.

Second, respect is necessary when it can be given with integrity. Muslims will not mention the Qur'an without qualifying it with an adjective like *sharif* (noble) nor mention one they consider a prophet without an honorific title. For Muslims from Iran on eastward it is commonly *hazrat* as in *Hazrat Ibrahim* (Abraham) or *Hazrat Muhammad*. In a dialogue in Kansas City I overheard a Muslim say he felt closer to the Christians because of their attitude of respect.

Third, an attitude of openness to new insights is required. Even my understanding of the Bible has been enriched by Muslims who understood some biblical and quranic themes better than I did.

Finally, trust should develop. My friend Professor Mahmoud Ayoub of Temple University and I were invited to Hartford Seminary to help evaluate their program. We argued about what should be done, then ate together, argued, then went to the hotel together. We trusted each other enough to speak our convictions.

Since both Christianity and Islam are missionary religions, mutual witness should be a natural part of authentic dialogue and need not be incompatible with empathetic and respectful listening. To affirm on both sides the desire that the other accept our understanding of God's revelation can enhance trust, because then there is less likelihood of hidden agendas.

The form and content of dialogue can be varied. Living and working together on common service projects, as I did with Muslims in an agricultural center in Lebanon, facilitates understanding. Doing fun things can be even better, such as regular eating together, an important aspect of friendship in most cultures. I attended a weekly interreligious dinner and discussion at the nearby Claremont Colleges, and my wife attends Arab association meetings. Shared experiences do not lend themselves to debate. These experiences can include being present when others worship and trying to feel the experience even while only personally participating to the extent that one can in good conscience and that those of the other faith feel is appropriate.

Dialogue of this inner spiritual nature can be enhanced by Muslims explaining their experiences. For example, a few years ago an Imam and his son explained their experience of fasting in a Cairo mosque to a Christian group of which I was a part. Dialogue can also involve sharing stories about what it is like to be nurtured in the other faith, as a group of Jews, Christians, and Muslims recently did in New Orleans.

Dialogue can often take place when focussed on a common concern, as in the U.S. Interreligious Committee for Peace in the Middle East, but this can be a mine field when emotions are deep and perspectives divergent.

The most conceptual or theological dialogues can be institutional. As a staff member of the Christian Study Center in Pakistan, I regularly participated in such a dialogue with the staff of the neighboring Islamic Research Institute. Or dialogue can include one faith community inviting a specialist from the other to speak. St. Peter's by the Sea, a church near Los Angeles, recently invited the director of the Islamic Center of Orange County and me to share in this way.

## Preparation for Dialogue

For People of the Book, as Jews and Christians are called in the Qur'an, it can be very helpful to get a biblical perspective on dialogue. This is important because of our legitimate fears of syncretism or relativism. A task force of which I was a part was commissioned by the Presbyterian Church (USA) to give guidance in such areas.

Passages in Hebrew Scriptures that support dialogue include: "You shall not bear false witness against your neighbor" (Ex. 20:16) and "Love your neighbor as yourself" (Lev. 19:18). As for the promise of relationship to God outside God's chosen people, there are many evidences—for example, the covenant after the flood (Gen. 9:16), the encounter of Abraham with Melchizedek (Gen. 14:18-19), and the greatness of God's name among the nations (Mal. 1:11).

Christians can also find additional support for God's truth and activity outside the church—for example, evidence of God in nature and in our conscience (Rom. 1 and 2); God "has not left himself without a witness" (Acts 14:16-17); and "in every nation anyone who fears him [the

Gentile 'God fearers'] and does what is right is acceptable to him" (Acts 10:34-35).

In addition, the value of dialogue should be explored. It corrects stereotypes and fosters understanding, communication, cooperation, and witness. Furthermore, it does not require the abandonment of belief in the uniqueness of one's own faith since dialogue involves authentic witness.

Many dialogues I have participated in have retrod the same ground. Therefore, there is value in studying the results of previous meetings in order to build on their conclusions.

The relative power of the communities in dialogue greatly influences the dynamics. Therefore, the stronger party locally needs to be sensitive to meet where the other feels secure. In the United States I usually offer to meet in the Muslim facility because of their minority position. Also, plans should be made together. Certain Muslim leaders in Kansas City have been especially sensitive to this kind of joint planning.

## Guidelines for Dialogue

The guidelines for dialogue include, first, each community's right to define its own position. One of my most profitable experiences was a day in Pakistan with a Muslim holy man. We each described our own faith in the presence of his disciples. Both of us were careful to speak only for ourselves.

Second, equals must be compared—the ideals of both faiths or the actual practice of each, not the formal faith of one with the folk practices of the other. The actual beliefs of individuals, however, can be very instructive. For example, though formal Islam denies the fatherhood of God, I have met Muslims who think of God like a father, hence are closer to a Christian understanding of God than orthodox literature would indicate.

A third guideline is to look for ways to avoid unnecessary confrontation. When pointing out what appear to me to be inadequacies in Islam, I often make the problem mine: "I have trouble with this" or "How do you deal with this?" Often I am asked questions like, "What do you think of Muhammad?" Knowing that part of my answer might offend, I might answer with a question like, "What would you think if I said a major prophet came after Muhammad?" Knowing they will affirm that Muhammad is the seal of the prophets, I can say that I feel the same way about Jesus. My point is made without saying anything negative that could be counterproductive.

In the neighboring town of San Marino recently an unfortunate statement was made about Arabs and reported in the newspaper. This could have led to an angry confrontation that also had some religious overtones; so my wife suggested that the Arab parents make a positive response and donate books to the school libraries that would explain ethnic and religious differences.

In like manner, rather than attacking Muslim governments in Afghanistan and Saudi Arabia for restrictions on religious freedom, when our family lived there I shared with government officials a strong case for tolerance and freedom from Muslim sources. Hesitancy to criticize another's position can be coupled with quickness to critique the history of one's own tradition. I have found this particularly true in justice and peace issues.

A fourth guideline is that building community facilitates the discussion of issues. This was evident while I worked with Muslims at an agricultural center in Lebanon. Relationships are built by letting Muslims be hosts or by borrowing an egg or stopping for coffee. They are also built by working for minority rights in our country, by empathizing with Muslim trauma in issues like the Salman Rushdie affair, and by trying to interpret their concerns to others.

Fifth, dialogues are facilitated by establishing agendas, parameters, and ground rules. In a recent interfaith dialogue in New Orleans, we moved toward goals as we observed these.

Sixth, interfaith experiences on many university campuses have  born out that dialogues progress more constructively when areas of agreement are explored before areas of disagreement, whether the concern is theological or practical.

A final guideline is to attempt to keep a balance in the number of participants and, if possible, in their gender. This minimizes feelings of defensiveness on the part of underrepresented individuals.

One of my most rewarding interfaith experiences resulted from a Pakistani Muslim scholar asking me: What is the chief purpose of humans?  From my tradition, I answered: "To glorify God and enjoy Him forever." After he asked what that meant, we set up a schedule to discuss my answer.  Through this interaction we both grew in our understanding of how we could glorify God and enjoy God, even while we continued to hope that the other would enter into our experience of God.

# JEWISH IDENTITY IN THE CHANGING WORLD OF AMERICAN RELIGION

## Jonathan D. Sarna

Efforts to foretell the future of the American Jewish community date far back to the nineteenth century, and for the most part the prophecies have been exceedingly gloomy. Former President John Adams predicted in a letter to Mordecai Noah in 1819 that Jews might "possibly in time become liberal Unitarian Christians." A young American Jewish student named William Rosenblatt, writing in 1872, declared that the grandchildren of Jewish immigrants to America would almost surely intermarry and abandon the rite of circumcision. Within fifty years "at the latest," he predicted, Jews would be "undistinguishable from the mass of humanity which surrounds them." Just under a century later, in 1964, *Look* magazine devoted a whole issue to the "Vanishing American Jew," at the time a much-discussed subject. More recently, in 1984, Rabbi Reuven Bulka, in a book entitled *The Orthodox-Reform Rift and the Future of the Jewish People*, warned that "we are heading towards a disaster of massive proportions which the North American Jewish community simply cannot afford." [1]

So far, thank God, all of these predictions have proven wrong. The Jewish people lives on. Some might consider this a timely reminder that (as someone once said) "prediction is very difficult, especially about the future." Others may view our continuing survival as nothing less than providential: evidence that God, in a display of divine mercy, is watching over us. A third view, my own, is that precisely because Jews are so worried about survival, we listen attentively to prophets of doom and respond to them. Gloom-and-doom prophets function historically as a kind of Jewish early-warning system: their Jeremiads hit home and produce necessary changes. For this reason, contemporary prophets, much like the biblical Jonah, are often fated to spend their lives as "self-negating prophets." Their widely publicized prophecies, instead of being fulfilled, usually result in the kinds of changes needed to "avert the evil decrees."

With this in mind, I should like to focus here on a basic change in the character of contemporary American religion that seems to me fraught with serious implications for American Jewish identity in the coming decades, and which is all too little discussed in professional Jewish circles. Specifically, my subject concerns the decline of the Judeo-Christian, Protestant-Catholic-Jew model of American religion, and the growth of non-Judeo-Christian religions, particularly Islam. While, broadly speaking, I see this development as part of a larger precess that Robert Wuthnow understands as nothing less than "the restructuring of American religion," [2] I am going to focus here on the subject at hand, and postpone discussion of other aspects of this "restructuring" for another occasion.

To understand the decline of the Judeo-Christian, Protestant-Catholic-Jew model of American religion requires first a brief excursion into history. For well over a century after the Constitution was promulgated, a great many Americans still believed that they lived in a Christian, often more narrowly defined as a Protestant country. The First Amendment did not bother those who held this view, for they believed, following Justice Joseph Story, that

> The real object of the amendment was not to countenance, much less to advance Mahometanism, or Judaism, or infidelity, by prostrating Christianity; but to exclude all rivalry among Christian sects, and to prevent any national ecclesiastical establishment, which should give to an hierarchy the exclusive patronage of the national government. [3]

"Christian America" advocates were also not bothered

by challenges from non-Christians. Given late-nineteenth-century figures showing that Protestant churches out-numbered all the others by a factor of more than ten to one, dissenters could be safely dismissed, if not altogether ignored. [4]

Even the Supreme Court agreed in 1892 that "this is a Christian nation." The justice who wrote that decision, David Brewer, the son of a missionary, subsequently defended his views in a widely published lecture unabashedly titled *The United States: A Christian Nation* (1905). [5] Jews certainly objected to this formulation, and consistently battled against the whole "Christian America" idea. But they did not make a great deal of headway. [6]

The more inclusive conception of America as a "Judeo-Christian" nation, referring to values or beliefs shared by Jews and Christians alike, developed only in the twentieth century, though adumbrations of it may be found a century or more earlier. Mark Silk, whose account I follow here, traces the contemporary use of this term to the 1930's. "What brought this usage into regular discourse," he writes, "was opposition to fascism. Fascist fellow travelers and anti-Semites had appropriated 'Christian' as a trademark...'Judeo-Christian' thus became a catchword for the other side." Using a wide range of examples from this period, Silk shows how "Judeo-Christian" gradually became the standard liberal term for the idea that Western values rested upon a shared religious consensus. "We speak now, with still inadequate but steadily expanding understanding, of the Judeo-Christian heritage," Hebrew Union College president Julian Morgenstern thus wrote in 1942. "We comprehend, as we have not comprehended in all of nineteen hundred years, that Judaism and Christianity are partners in the great work of world-redemption and the progressive unfolding of the world-spirit." Ten years later, President-elect Dwight D. Eisenhower spoke of the "Judeo-Christian concept" that formed the basis of "our form of government." "As of 1952," Silk concludes, "good Americans were supposed to be good Judeo-Christians. It was the new national creed."[7]

Side by side with this creed, there developed in America a new and more pluralistic model of how the nation's religious character should be conceptualized and described. Earlier, the standard textbooks, from Robert Baird's *Religion in America* (1843) to William Warren Sweet's *Story of Religion in America* (1930), adhered to what might be called the "Protestant synthesis"; they were overwhelmingly concerned, as Sydney Ahlstrom points out, with "the rise and development of the Protestant tradition."[8] With the twentieth-century decline of mainline Protestantism, the remarkable growth of Catholicism, the interreligious assault on wartime and postwar hatred, the rise of the interfaith movement, and the coming of age of non-Protestant intellectuals, this synthesis broke down. In place of the "Protestant tradition" paradigm, there arose a new tripartite model of American religion, the familiar trinity of Protestant, Catholic, and Jew.

As early as 1920, before this ideology had fully crystallized, "leaders of the Protestant, Catholic and Jewish groups united in an appeal to the people of America to help safeguard religious liberty from the menace of bigotry, prejudice and fanaticism." Seven years later, the National Conference of Jews and Christians was established (the name was changed in 1938-39), and by design it had three co-chairmen: Newton D. Baker, Protestant; Carlton J. H. Hayes, Catholic; and Roger W. Straus, Jew. The NCCJ's education program featured hundreds of local "round tables," each one "a body of Protestant, Catholic and Jewish leaders" who joined together "to further the aims of the National Conference in its community." Everett R. Clinchy, the NCCJ's longtime executive director, soon developed this idea into a full-scale ideology, arguing that America consisted of three coequal "culture groups," each of which made valuable contributions to American life and should be encouraged to flourish. Within two decades, this tripartite approach to American religion was enshrined in countless symbols, from "equal-time" on radio allotments on NBC to the famous Chapel of Four Chaplains, "an interfaith shrine" commemorating the 1943 sinking death—"standing on deck, arms linked, praying"—of four army chaplains, one Catholic, one Jewish, and two Protestant, on the *S.S. Dorchester*. [9]

What did more than anything else to make "Protestant-Catholic-Jew" a household concept was a book that appeared in 1955. Written by Will Herberg, recently characterized by David G. Dalin as "one of the most interesting Jewish intellectuals of the last half-century," it made the case for "the pervasivenes of religious self-identification along the tripartite scheme of Protestant, Catholic, Jew." According to Herberg, America had become a " 'triple melting pot,' restructured in three great communities with religious labels, defining three great 'communions' or 'faiths.'" "Not to be...either a Protestant, a Catholic, or a Jew," he warned, "is somehow not to be an American." [10]

By the mid-1950's, then, both the Judeo-Christian tradition and the "triple melting pot" had become firmly entrenched components of American identity. Both models—and they were clearly linked—pointed to a more pluralistic understanding of America, an America that embraced Jews as equals. For Jews, all too used to being cast in the role of persecuted minority, this was a pleasant change. Indeed, it was so congenial that in a paper entitled "The Basic Task of the Synagogue in America," the Conservative Jewish lay leader Maxwell Abbell matter-of-factly read these assumptions back into history. "Americans," he explained, "have always spoken of the Judeo-Christian traditions as the basis of the religious life of the modern world, thus giving us Jews credit for the basic elements of this tradition. Americans have always spoken of the three great religions of this country as Protestantism, Catholicism and Judaism, despite the fact that we Jews number only about five million out of about 160 million population." [11]

Abbell, and I think many other Jews as well, understood that Jews did not quite deserve the coequal status that America accorded them. They apparently hoped that Jews might compensate for their manifest numerical inequality by making a substantial contribution to American life. But there was a great danger here that I think we are only now beginning to appreciate: namely, that there was a large and indeed growing disjunction between myth and reality. Neither the Judeo-Christian tradition nor the "triple melting pot" adequately or accurately conveyed the full extent of American religious pluralism in all of its complex manifestations. For a long time, Americans lived with this disjunction, cognitive dissonance notwithstanding. Jews found their exaggerated status particularly convenient; an overwhelming number of Americans believed that Jews formed a far larger proportion of the nation's population than they actually did, and treated Jews accordingly. [12] But today these myths are dying. It behooves us to know why they are dying, and what the implications are for Jewish identity in the coming decades.

Mark Silk demonstrates that the Judeo-Christian idea first met with resistance as far back as the 1940's. Criticisms included the charge that the concept was fuzzy (Harvard's Douglas Bush, for one, asked for "fuller hints of what the Hebraic-Christian tradition, to which all pay at least vague lip service, actually does or can mean in modern terms for modern men of good will"), and that it obscured age-old Jewish-Christian differences. The concept was further attacked in the wake of the 1967 Six-Day War, an event that exposed deep theological fissures between Jews and Christians, especially with regard to Israel, and hastened a trend towards greater Jewish self-pride. More recently, "Judeo-Christian" has been attacked as a rhetorical ploy used by right-wing elements in order to promote an exclusively Christian political program. [13]

The so-called triple melting pot proved no more adequate as an explanatory concept. It seriously underestimated the importance of ethnic differences, totally misunderstood the significance of Evangelical Protestantism, and wrote off other American faiths completely, as if they did not exist at all. David Dalin points out that "even as Herberg was writing, new evangelical sects were arising and older ones were undergoing revitalization. Less than five years after the publication of *Protestant-Catholic-Jew*, the sociologist Seymour Martin Lipset could note that such fundamentalist sects were 'far stronger today than at any time in the 20th century,' and that the much-heralded growth in church membership was taking place precisely among theses 'fringe sects,' rather than within the tradition Protestant 'mainline' denominations in which Herberg placed so much stock." [14] Admittedly, Herberg's model did help pave the way for subsequent discussions of American "civil religion." But the triple melting pot by itself was scarcely an adequate depiction of American religion in the 1950's, and was even less adequate thereafter.

Today, assumptions about America's Judeo-Christian character and its Protestant-Catholic-Jew makeup confront an even more critical problem: the rapid growth of American religions that are not Protestant, Catholic, or Jewish, and are totally outside the Judeo-Christian spectrum. I refer principally to Islam, among the fastest-growing religions in the United States, but we should also bear in mind the presence in America of so-called hidden religions (the term is J. Gordon Melton's), including metaphysical faiths, Eastern religions, Psychic or New Age religions, and the like. Sociologists Wade Clark Roof and William McKinney found in 1985 that non-Judeo-Christian faiths commanded the loyalty of twice as many Americans as Judaism and that nearly one American in ten reported no religious affiliation. In other words, at least thirteen percent of all Americans do not fit our standard assumptions about America's religious character. This presents more than a fourfold increase in just thirty years, and there is every reason to believe that the number of these "exceptions" will continue to expand at a rapid rate. [15]

From the point of view of American Jews, the growth of American Islam merits special attention, especially given the organized Muslim community's hostility to Israel. Islam's emergence as a major American faith has failed until now to elicit much discussion in Jewish circles, probably from a fear of appearing religiously prejudiced. I am not familiar with a single scholarly study of what this development means to Jews, certainly none that investigates how Islam's rise may affect Jewish identity and life in the decades ahead. No detailed study can be attempted here either, but given my topic, "Jewish Identity in the Changing World of American Religion," some preliminary remarks are in order.

Historically, individual Muslims came to America as early as the colonial period. Small numbers of Muslims are known to have lived in various communities in the nineteenth century, but always as individuals; there was no organized Islamic presence. During the era of mass immigration (1880s-World War I), migration from what was then called Greater Syria increased owing to a wide variety of factors: political and economic insecurity, agricultural problems, overpopulation, the decline of the Ottoman Empire, and the lure of economic advancement in the New World. Most of the immigrants were actually Christian Arabs, but a number of Muslims came too— "they hoped to earn as much as possible and then return home." [16] The oft-told story of the small Muslim community established near Ross, North Dakota around 1900 demonstrates the difficulties that Muslims faced in a non-Muslim environment. To Jewish ears, the story sounds remarkably familiar.

> Before a mosque was built in the 1920s, prayer and ritual were conducted in private houses and led by the best informed among the group. Without a mosque for almost thirty years and without any cultural reinforcement from newcomers, the Muslims rapidly lost the use of Arabic, assumed Christian names, and married non-Muslims. The community dwindled as children moved away, and the mosque was abandoned by 1948. [17]

The most visible early centers of Islam in America were

in Michigan, especially in the Detroit and Dearborn areas, for many Arab immigrants took jobs at the Ford plant. Other Muslim communities were established in East Coast and Midwest industrial centers. But given immigration restrictions and assimilation, the number of Muslims in America remained small—"a little over 100,000"—into the early 1960s. Since then, the nation's Islamic population has mushroomed, owing both to large scale immigration (fourteen percent of all immigrants in the United States are now Muslims) and to thousands of converts, especially blacks. Significant Islamic communities may be found in New York, Los Angeles, Chicago, Detroit, and Toledo, Ohio. One recent study lists 598 mosques and Islamic centers operating in the United States, and estimates the number of American Muslims as "somewhere in the range of two to three million"—a conservative estimate. [18] "The high rate of birth, the growing number of converts, and the continuing flow of immigration," the study's authors conclude, "make it possible to predict that by the first decade of the twenty-first century Islam will be the second largest religious community in the United States." [19]

The Muslim community stands in the forefront of those who seek to break down the Judeo-Christian, Protestant-Catholic-Jew models of American religious life. Quite understandably, Muslim leaders feel that these models are exclusivistic; they imply that Muslims cannot participate as equals in American society. "We'd like people to start thinking of the U.S. as a Judeo-Christian-Muslim society," said Salam Al-Marayati, spokesman for the Muslim Political Action Committee. Another Muslim told researchers that he looked forward to the day "when all will say 'Catholics, Protestants, Jews and Muslims.'" [20] While such a change would not go far enough for those Muslims whose ultimate goal is to bring about an Islamic state in America, and would certainly not meet the needs of those whose faith is neither Judeo-Christian nor Muslim, it does bear out our earlier analysis. America's religious identity is changing; the way Jews understand

American religion must change as well.

What are the implications of these changes for American Jews and American Jewish identity? Given what we have seen to be the rather poor results of earlier efforts to foretell American Jewry's future, I might be forgiven if, echoing Amos, I declared myself to be neither a prophet nor a prophet's disciple, and left it at that. But since I want to pay special attention, at the very least, to the policy implications of my analysis, let me suggest ten possible changes that we may see in the years ahead, bearing in mind my earlier caution concerning self-negating prophecies. Some of these changes relate broadly to the new world of American religion that Jews must confront; the rest deal more narrowly with the growth of Islam, and its possible ramifications.

1. The one-time familiar trinity of Protestants, Catholics, and Jews will, in the future, almost surely give way to a much wider religious circle. At the very least, we shall have to include Muslims in the company of religious insiders; more likely, we shall have to expand the circle to include the full range of American religious denominations, Eastern religions as well as Western ones.

2. Our image of American religion will have to change to comport more closely than it now does with statistical realities. As such, Jews may find themselves placed on an equal footing not with Protestants and Catholics, but, ironically, with Muslims, for both represent major world religions comprising less than 3 percent of the total U.S. population. A hint of what lies in store may already be found in J. Gordon Melton's *Encyclopedia of American Religions* (1978). The encyclopedia claims to explore "the broad sweep of American religions and describes 1200 churches." It divides American religion into seventeen "religious families," only ten of which basically follow Christian beliefs and practices. Jews do not even rate a religious family of their own in this classification; instead they are grouped together with Muslims, Hindus, and Buddhists under "the Eastern

and Middle Eastern Family." "The inclusion here of the Jews, Hindus, Buddhists and Muslims in one family," J. Gordon Melton explains, "is based on shared characteristics, peculiar to their American sojourn, without negating their fundamental differences." [21]

3. Given the move away from the triple melting pot view of American religion, and the almost inevitable devaluation of Judaism's place in the panoply of American religion, Jews in the next few decades will have to endure what mainstream Protestants went through earlier in this century: the experience of status-loss, of feeling almost dispossessed. The rise in status that Jews experienced when the triple melting pot image gained ascendancy will, I believe, be partially if not wholly reversed. As a result, the Jewish community will have to learn how to live with a radically different image of itself—a much less flattering one.

4. As a consequence of all of the above, American Jews will receive far less textbook and media attention than they do now. Where for some years Jew benefitted from a disproportionate share of religious attention, almost on a par with Protestants and Catholics, now they will have to adjust their expectations down to a more realistic level in keeping with the Jewish community's actual size and significance.

5. Jewish political power in the years ahead may also fall into decline. As politicians become aware of America's changing religious situation, many may feel less inclined to listen when Jewish lobbyists come calling. Political power in America is, of course, more than just a function of numbers; organization, intelligence, experience, participation, and money also count for a great deal. But given countervailing pressure from constituents actively hostile to Jewish interests, the knowledge that America's Jews are a less significant group than they used to be cannot but have some impact. In the coming years, Jews will have to work much harder to achieve their goals and will not be able to take their power so much for granted.

6. Israel may well suffer the most from these changes. The declining status of American Jews, coupled with the rise of American Islam and the growing political maturity of the American Muslim community, will make it much more difficult in the years ahead for massive aid to Israel to win congressional approval. Already, the Muslim Political Action Committee is promoting pro-Palestinian policies. Having learned much from watching how Jewish political lobbyists work, American Muslims intend to increase their political activities in coming elections, and hoped to elect a Muslim to Congress by 1992. [22]

7. For a few decades, at least, we are likely to see a return in this country to the rhetoric of religious triumphalism. Faiths new on the American scene and flush with fresh converts often delude themselves into thinking that theirs is the faith of the future, the religion that will bring The Truth to all Americans and unite them in a single all-embracing church (or mosque). Almost inevitably, this pious hope stirs up religious fervor, spurs the faithful to participate in religious crusades, and successfully thwarts liberal efforts aimed at promoting interreligious harmony. Catholics, Jews, and mainstream Protestants know from experience that sooner or later all such hopes are doomed to disappointment; religious monism is not the American way. But this may well be the kind of lesson that every faith community must learn anew for itself.

8. Until this and other lessons *are* learned, interfaith conversations will become much more difficult. In the past, leading Jews, Protestants, and Catholics have, if nothing else, established certain properties that permitted them to interact; they all learned to practice what John Murray Cuddihy calls "the religion of civility." [23] Faiths previously excluded from the mainstream do not necessarily share these proprieties, and may in some cases openly scorn them—witness the intemperate rhetoric of some fundamentalist preachers or of Black Muslim leaders like Louis Farrakhan. Unless

(or until) a new generation of religious leaders from a much broader spectrum of faiths can be initiated into the niceties of religious conversation, progress can scarcely be expected. Discussions will either prove too limited to be meaningful or too acrimonious to be helpful.

9. On the brighter side, the rise of Islam and the widening parameters of American religion may in the long run promote closer Muslim-Jewish relations. Confronted with surprisingly similar kinds of religious problems in a society that is still overwhelmingly Christian, Jews and Muslims have every reason to learn to work together in support of common interests. Moreover, the neutral American environment should make possible a level of religious interaction between Jews and Muslims that would be unthinkable either in Arab countries or in Israel. For reasons that I have already outlined, I do not expect serious interreligious conversations to take place in the near future. But the history of Catholic-Jewish relations over the past century in America demonstrates that change is possible. Given what Robert Wuthnow writes about the "decline of denominationalism" [24] in recent decades, improvements may come about even sooner than we think.

10. Finally, the changing world of American religion may prompt Jews fundamentally to reevaluate their agenda and goals for the years ahead. If Jews are to be known once more as a religious minority, a so-called dissenting faith, they may want to act the part, just as they did decades ago. This means that Jews would focus first and foremost on their own interests, next on those issues of special concern for religious minorities, and only third on the great social and political agenda that majority faiths worry about. Historically, the Jewish community played a tremendously important role as leader and spokesman for America's religious minorities. It did more than any other faith community to promote inclusive theories of American life (the melting pot and cultural pluralism) and religious liberty for

all. Jews, in my opinion, have had far less impact as yea-saying members of the religious majority, and have squandered precious resources on issues about which they have little new to say. By refocusing priorities back toward minority-group issues—particularly the age-old American question of minority rights versus majority rule—Jews may actually make more of a mark than they did as members of the religious "establishment." Such a refocusing would not only strengthen Jewish minority-group identity, but would also have the additional advantage of promoting group survival as a weapon against intermarriage and assimilation.

Let me close with this final thought. Jews have done exceedingly well in this country, both in the old days when they were viewed as members of a religious minority roughly akin to Turks and infidels, and more recently when they became part of the religious majority, grouped together with Protestants and Catholics in a "triple melting pot." The fact that yet another change is now taking place should thus occasion concerned vigilance, but not necessarily alarm. Indeed, we have seen that some of the implications of this change may actually turn out to be positive. Moreover, it is a mistake to assume that Jews are merely the objects of history, tossed about by forces totally beyond their control. While Jews may not be able to do anything about the realignment of American religion and the growth of American Islam, the way the respond to these challenges may in fact make a great deal of difference. American Jews survive earlier challenges, prophecies of doom notwithstanding, because Jewish leaders responded to them creatively—with wisdom, discernment, and flexibility. Let us hope that our present leaders can do as well.

---

1.    John Adams to M. M. Noah (March 15, 1819), reprinted in Moshe Davis, *With Eyes Toward Zion* (New York: Arno, 1977), p. 19; W. M. Rosenblatt, "The Jews: What Are They Coming To," *Galaxy* 13 (January 1872): 60; Thomas B. Morgan; "The Vanishing American Jew," *Look* 28 (May 5, 1964): 42-46; Reuven P. Bulka, *The Coming Cataclysm* (Oakville, Ont.: Mosaic Press, 1984), p. 14; see also Stephen J. Whitfield, *American Space, Jewish Time* (Hamden, Conn.: Archon Books, 1988), pp. 171-191.

2. Robert Wuthnow, *The Restructuring of American Religion: Society and Faith Since World War II* (Princeton: Princeton University Press, 1988).

3. Joseph Story, *Commentaries on the Constitution of the United States* (Boston, 1833), as reprinted in John F. Wilson and Donald L. Drakeman, *Church and State in American History* (Boston, 1987), pp. 92-93.

4. Robert T. Handy, *A Christian America: Protestant Hopes and Historical Realities* (New York: Oxford, 1971), p. 118.

5. Morton Borden, *Jews, Turks and Infidels* (Chapel Hill: University of North Carolina Press, 1984), pp. 62-74; Naomi W. Cohen, *Encounter with Emancipation: The German Jews in the United States, 1830-1914* (Philadelphia: Jewish Publication Society, 1984), pp. 98-100, 254-256.

6. Jonathan D. Sarna, *American Jews and Church-State Relations: The Search for "Equal Footing"* (New York: American Jewish Committee, 1989), esp. pp. 4-10.

7. Mark Silk, *Spiritual Politcs: Religion and America Since World War I* (New York: Simon & Schuster, 1988), pp. 40-53. Silk provides numerous other quotations from this period in addition to the ones I have used here. See also Silk's "Notes on the Judeo-Christian Tradition in America," *American Quarterly* 36 (Spring 1984): 65-85. In a forthcoming article, Benny Kraut will argue that the Judeo-Christian concept actually arose in the 1920s as a part of that decade's interreligious "goodwill" movement. I am grateful to Prof. Kraut for sharing his material with me prior to publication.

8. Sydney E. Ahlstrom, *A Religious History of the American People* (New Haven: Yale University Press, 1972), pp. 8-12; see also R. Laurence Moore, *Religious Outsiders and the Making of Americans* (New York: Oxford, 1986); and more broadly Henry W. Bowden, "The Historiography of American Religion," in *Encyclopedia of the American Religious Experience*, ed. Charles H. Lippy and Peter W. Williams (New York: Charles Scribner's Sons, 1987), vol. 1, pp. 3-16.

9. Everett R. Clinchy, "Better Understanding," *Universal Jewish Encyclopedia* (1942) vol. 2, p. 257; Louis Minsky, "National Conference of Christians and Jews," ibid., vol. 8, p. 114; Benny Kraut, "Towards the Establishment of the National Conference of Christians and Jews: The Tenuous Road to Religious Goodwill in the 1920s," *American Jewish History* 77, no. 3 (March 1988): 388-412; idem, "A Wary Collaboration: Jews, Catholics and the Protestant Goodwill Movement" (forthcoming); Alex J. Goldman, "Alexander D. Goode," in *Giants of the Faith: Great American Rabbis* (New York, 1964), pp. 311-329; see also Lance J. Sussman " 'Toward Better Understanding': The Rise of the Interfaith Movement in America and the Role of Rabbi Isaac Landman," *American Jewish Archives* 34 (April 1982): 35-51.

10. Will Herberg, *Protestant-Catholic-Jew: An Essay in American Religious Sociology*, rev. ed. (New York: Anchor Books, 1960), esp. pp. 256-257; David G. Dalin, "Will Herberg in Retrospect," *Commentary* 86 (July 1988): 38-43.

11. Maxwell Abbell, "The Basic Task of the Synagogue in America," *Torch*, Winter 1955, reprinted in Milton Berger et al., *Roads to Jewish Survival* (New York: Bloch, 1967), p. 153.

12. Charles H. Stember et al., *Jews in the Mind of America* (New York: Basic Books, 1966), p. 77.

13. Silk, *Spiritual Politcs*, pp. 42-44, 142-146, 180.

14. Dalin, "Will Herberg in Retrospect," p. 42.

15. Wade Clark Roof and William McKinney, *American Mainline Religion: Its Changing Shape and Future* (New Brunswick, N.J., 1987), esp. p. 17; Silk, *Spiritual Politics*, p. 181; for an exhaustive survey of non-Judeo-Christian reli-

gions, see G. Gordon Melton, *TheEncyclopedia of American Religions* (Wilmington, N. C.: McGrath Publishing Co., 1978, 1985). These "exceptions," it should be stressed, are not for the most part avowed secularists. Americans are simply defining religion in ways that they rarely if ever did before. For a valuable compilation of survey data regarding *"Unsecular America,"* see Richard J. Neuhaus, ed., *Unsecular America* (Grand Rapids, Mich.: Erdmans, 1986), esp. pp. 115-158.

16. Anthony B. Toth, " The Syrian Community in New Castle and Its Unique Alawi Component, 1900-1940," W*estern Pennsylvania Historical Magazine* 69 (July 1986): 221-239; Newell S. Booth Jr. , "Islam in North America, " *Encyclopedia of the American Religious Experience*, ed. Charles H. Lippy and Peter W. Williams (New York: Charles Scribner's Sons, 1987), vol. 2, p. 725. For earlier sources, see George Dimitri Selim, comp., *The Arabs in the United States: A Selected List of References*, Mideast Directions bibliographies of the Library of Congress (Washington, 1983).

17. Alixa Naff, "Arabs," in *Harvard Encyclopedia of American Ethnic Groups*, ed. Stephen Thernstrom et al. (Cambridge, Mass.: Harvard University Press, 1980), p. 132.

18. Yvonne Yazbeck Haddad and Adair T. Lummis, *Islamic Values in the United States* (New York: Oxford, 1987), p. 3. *Time*, May 23, 1988, p. 49, quotes Carol Stone's estimate of 4,644,000 Muslims, and *New York Times*, February 21, 1989, p. 1, speaks of "6 million Muslims in the United States."

19. Haddad and Lummis, *Islamic Values in the United States*, p. 3; *Time*, May 23, 1988, p. 49, makes the same point: "U. S. Muslims are expected to surpass Jews in number and, in less than 30 years, become the country's second largest religious community, after Christians."

20. *Time*, May 23, 1988, p. 50: Haddad and Lummis, *Islamic Values in the United States*, p. 161.

21. Melton, *Encyclopedia of American Religions*, vol. 1, pp. vii-xii; vol. 2, pp. 307-354. Melton's idiosyncratic classification scheme is, of course, easy to criticize. His depiction of American Judaism is filled with gross errors, and his inclusion of Jews for Jesus under "Mainstream Judaism" is offensive.

22. *Time*, August 23, 1988, p. 50. Writing in the wake of the Six-Day War, the Arab sociologist Abdo A. Elkholy dreamed of a far more radical agenda for Arab Americans. "Many of the great national movements which have changed the course of our modern history started abroad," he pointed out. "Could it be that future historians will focus on the Arab elites in America and their role in a sweeping Arab revolution which would unify the Middle East and liberate it from both international Zionism and military domination and corruption?" See Abdo A. Elkholy, "The Arab-Americans: Nationalism and Traditionalism and Traditional Preservations," in *The Arab Americans: Studies in Assimilation*, ed. Elaine C. Hagopian and Ann Paden (Wilmette, Ill: Medina University Press, 1969) p. 17.

23. John Murray Cuddihy, *No Offense: Civil Religion and Protestant Taste* (New York: Seabury, 1978).

24. Wuthnow, *Restructuring of American Religion*, pp. 71-99.

# ABRAHAM: THE FIRST JEW OR THE FIRST MUSLIM?[1] TEXT, TRADITION, AND "TRUTH" IN INTERRELIGIOUS DIALOGUE

## Reuven Firestone

It has become increasingly clear in this country during the past decade that the religious tradition and civilization of Islam must be taken more seriously.[2] The slow but nevertheless noticeable movement in American thinking is due to two major factors: the growing realization that the instability in the Middle East will adversely affect the well-being of our own country, and the growing numbers and visibility of the Muslim community in the United States. The great numbers of Americans stationed in the Arabian Peninsula during the 1991 Gulf War, and the integration of forces between Arab countries and the West has further increased American curiosity about Islam. One result of these developments has been an increase in dialogue groups seeking Muslim participants. This essay will examine several aspects of the Jewish and Islamic Abraham stories which will shed light on issues associated with applying approaches of comparative religion to interreligious dialogue.[3]

Any comparison of the three great monotheistic religions reveals extensive parallels and similarities at the same time that it discloses many distinctions and disagreements. At the most basic level, for example, all three religious systems require worship of the one God. Moreover, they each derive the authority of their religious systems through scripture and its interpretation and they even revere common legends and personalities. A careful examination of the commonalities confirms the great number of apparent textual, theological, and legal parallels, but it also reveals that many, if not most, seemingly identical traditions are actually significantly at variance. Perhaps the most basic and revealing case would be that of Abraham, to whom we often point as the common ancestor of all three major monotheistic faiths. While it is true that Abraham is indeed regarded by each religious system as its progenitor and role model, each tends to see Abraham in such a different light that one is forced to ask in many cases whether they are referring to the same person.

## Abraham in the Qur'an

According to the biblical account, Abraham left Ur of the Chaldees with his father Terah and journeyed to Haran where his father died. From Haran, he journeyed along with his wife Sarah and nephew lot to Eretz Kena'an—the Land of the peoples of Canaan—in response to God's command. Aside from a brief sojourn in Egypt, the Bible depicts Abraham thereafter living a nomadic life in or adjacent to the land promised by God to him and his offspring and known later as Eretz Yisra'el—the Land of the Israelites. [4] While in Egypt, according to Jewish tradition but not explicitly mentioned in the biblical text, Hagar was given as a handmaid to Abraham's wife, Sarah. [5]

Abraham and Sarah proceed to have a number of adventures, but they remain childless. When it has become quite clear by Genesis 16 that Sarah is past childbearing age, she gives her Egyptian handmaid to Abraham so that he might attain an heir through her. Soon after Hagar becomes pregnant a terrible conflict ensues between the two women. Sarah, the woman with higher social status, treats Hagar so harshly that the latter flees into the desert where she meets an angel of God. The angel commands her to return to Sarah and gives Hagar a somewhat enigmatic prophecy regarding her future son, Ishmael, who will be aggressive and independent, as will be his innumerable progeny with which he is blessed. Hagar returns and Ishmael is born.

In chapter 17, the covenant between Abraham and God is reaffirmed through the act of circumcision. Ishmael is circumcised along with Abraham's entire male household. God also promises Abraham a son through Sarah, and informs him that the covenant will attain only through Sarah's son Isaac—not through Ishmael. God nevertheless assures Abraham that Ishmael will also father a great nation, begetting twelve princes.

When the story zooms in on Isaac's birth in chapter 21, we learn that Abraham and Sarah's son is circumcised, but during the weaning celebration occurring a year or so later, the conflict still smoldering between Sarah and Hagar bursts forth into a conflagration. Sarah insists upon banishing Hagar and her son from the family unit. Abraham is deeply saddened by this, but God instructs him nevertheless to follow Sarah's wishes. So he rises early on the day of their departure in order to send them off with provisions which are eventually spent in the desert.

Hagar sets Ishmael down under a bush and walks far enough away that she will not hear the cries of her son dying of thirst, for she cannot bear the pain. She sits down and cries bitterly; God hears the voice of Ishmael and sends an angel who confirms the divine promise that Ishmael will become a great nation. God provides a miraculous well for them and continues to provide for the boy as he grows up in the wilderness of Paran.

This is essentially the end of Ishmael's story in the Bible. A brief comment can be found in Genesis 25:9, where after Abraham's death, Ishmael and Isaac join together to bury their father. The names of Ishmael's twelve sons are also provided here, along with the statement that Ishmael lived to the age of 137. A few scattered references note that a desert people known as *Yishma'elim* (Ishmaelites) do indeed continue to live in adjacent lands [6] but nothing more can be found of Ishmael in the Bible.

He disappears after his removal from the sacred history of God's covenant with Israel.

According to the revelation of the Qur'an, however, Abraham's relationship with Ishmael does not end at Hagar and Ishmael's banishment. Abraham personally settles some of his progeny at the site of the holy city of Mecca. He and Ishmael build God's House (the Ka'ba) there and purify it for religious ritual, and Abraham is credited with calling all of humanity to make the Hajj or sacred Pilgrimage to the holy sites in and around Mecca. [7]

Because the Qur'an is not organized by chronology as is most of the Bible, references to Abraham and Ishmael are scattered through some two dozen chapters in a variety of contexts. Qur'an 14:37 mentions that Abraham brought some of his offspring to live in an uncultivated valley next to God's sacred House (*'inda baytikal-muharram*) in order to establish regular prayer. The location of that sacred place is not given in this reference. Qur'an 3:96, however, mentions that the first house of worship provided for humankind was at the blessed Bakka—a synonym, say Muslim commentators, for the holy city of Mecca (written and pronounced in Arabic as Makka). [8] The Qur'an continues in the following verse to tell us that the famous *Maqám Ibráhim*—the Station of Abraham— is located there, and indeed, there is a Station of Abraham in Mecca today within the Sacred Compound in which lies the Ka'ba, the inviolable ritual center of Islam. The Qur'an tells us further that this is the place to which Pilgrimage, the Hajj, is a religious obligation. In fact, in Qur'an 2:124-129, we learn how Abraham and Ishmael raised up the foundations of the Ka'ba and purified it for the Pilgrimage and for prayer.

The Qur'an does not, however, explain how Abraham came to Mecca. It rather assumes that its audience already knows the answer. And, indeed, traditional Islamic exegesis recalls ancient legends telling of Abraham's journey from the Holy Land near Jerusalem to the Holy Land of Mecca and its environs. [9] The legend that follows can be found in the most authoritative Qur'an commentaries. It is generally cited on the authority of one of the most respected early Qur'an commentators and a personal companion of Muhammad, 'Abdalláh Ibn' Abbás. [10]

Although no biblical verses are quoted nor is the Bible ever referred to directly, the legend is quite familiar to those acquainted with the conflict between Sarah and Hagar as depicted in Genesis 16 and 21. As in Genesis 21:14, the Islamic telling depicts Abraham giving Hagar provisions for the journey. But unlike the biblical account, the Islamic rendering has Abraham accompany Hagar and Ishmael in order to personally bring them to the deserted site of the future holy city of Mecca. [11] Abraham leaves them under a scrubby tree next to the location of the Ka'ba, reminiscent of Hagar leaving Ishmael under the bush in Genesis 21:15. Abraham then sets out for the long journey back toward Jerusalem, but Hagar follows and asks to whom Abraham is entrusting them in such a desolate place. After a long silence, he answers, "to God," and before embarking on his return journey, Abraham recites this prayer found in Qur'an 14:37: "O Lord! I have made some of my offspring live in an uncultivated valley by your Sacred House, in order, O Lord, that they establish regular prayer."

Ishmael is only an infant at the time. When the water in Hagar's waterskin is depleted, she becomes dehydrated and her milk stops flowing for her son. As Ishmael's thirst becomes unbearable, he begins writhing in the throes of death. Hagar cannot bear to see him die, so she leaves him under the bush (Cf. Gen. 21:16) and climbs a nearby hill to look for help. When none is to be found, she runs across to the opposite hill and urgently looks from there as well, but sees nothing. She runs desperately between the hills seven times, and just as hope appears lost, she hears a voice. She runs back to her son whom she sees is now accompanied by an angel, often named in the texts as Gabriel. He miraculously brings forth water from the ground for them and Hagar immediately scoops it into her waterskin, thus saving the life of her son (Cf. Genesis

16:7f and 21:17-20). The angel tells Hagar that the boy and his father will one day build the House of God at that very spot.

According to Islam, this story provides the sacred origin of the hallowed Zamzam well, the very well within today's sacred precinct at Mecca from which pilgrims still drink when they make the Meccan Pilgrimage. The hills between which Hagar ran searching for help are the sacred hills of Safa and Marwa, and every Muslim pilgrim ritually re-enacts Hagar's running between them seven times even today.

The story is not over, however, for after Hagar and Ishmael are established in Mecca, a group of Arabs from the ancient tribe of Jurhum happens by and notices signs of life in what was thought to be a dry and deserted valley. They send a scout who finds Hagar and Ishmael near the miraculous well. When they see the fecundity of the blessed spring, the tribal leaders ask permission of Hagar to settle with her there. Permission is granted, and the Jurhum bring their families to Mecca, thereby establishing a settlement in that sacred place. As Ishmael grows up, he learns the Arabic language and culture from the Jurhum tribe and eventually marries one of their women.

This might seem an appropriate ending to the legend but in fact it continues, for Abraham is not satisfied that he left his son alone with Hagar in the desert, despite the fact that he knows God will be with the boy (as in Genesis 21:20). As a loving and responsible father who has not rejected his eldest son, he feels the need to visit him in order to see personally how he is faring, so he journeys to Mecca. [12] Ishmael is away from home at the time so Abraham meets only his rude and inhospitable wife. As a result of their unpleasant meeting, Abraham tells her to give her husband a coded message that Ishmael should divorce her. Abraham then proceeds on his return journey northward without seeing Ishmael. When Ishmael returns he immediately senses that his father had been there and asks his wife what happened. She innocently tells him about a strange old man who suddenly came upon them, and Ishmael knows from the coded message behind her words that he must divorce her. The dutiful son immediately divorces his wife and then marries another women from the Jurhum tribe.

Abraham once again feels the need to visit his son, but upon his arrival Ishmael is again away. On this occasion, however, Abraham is received with wonderful hospitality and respect by Ishmael's new wife (note how Abraham represents the very epitome of hospitality for both Judaism and Islam). Abraham once more asks Ishmael's wife to give her husband a coded message, but this time she is confirmed as the proper martial choice. They have children, and through a long genealogy not provided in this legend but connected to the legend by other Islamic sources, it becomes clear that the ultimate result of this divinely sanctioned match (through the intervention of God's prophet Abraham) is the birth of Muhammad, the last and greatest of all God's true prophets.

Abraham later visits Mecca a third time. This time he finds Ishmael at home, trimming arrows in the shade of the same tree under which Abraham had left him and his mother so many years before. Abraham informs Ishmael that God had given him a command. Ishmael replies that if God had commanded anything to Abraham, he is obligated to carry it out. Abraham then informs Ishmael of God's command to them both to build the holy Ka'ba, as in Qur'an 2:127. They dutifully obey the divine decree, and Ishmael hands his father the stones as Abraham sets them in place on the sacred structure. As they build, they pray the verse found in Qur'an 2:127:

"Our Lord, accept [this] from us, for you are the all-hearing, the all-knowing."

## Biblical vs. Qur'anic History

The Jewish and the Islamic sources of the Abraham-

Ishmael legend represent two different—and in many respects contradictory—versions of sacred history, each based upon a different sacred scripture. According to the biblical view, God's covenant with Abraham is established with Isaac, not with the rejected Ishmael. Isaac's son Jacob is subsequently renamed Israel by God's angel, and he fathers the twelve tribes that will make up the Israelite people. The covenant is established with Isaac—not Ishmael. Isaac is a willing sacrifice to God on Mt. Moriah, the very location of the future Temple in Jerusalem: God's House. Abraham's progeny through Isaac will eventuate in David, the greatest king of Israel, and the symbol for the unity and future messianic redemption of the Jewish people.

But according to the Islamic view, Abraham personally brings his oldest son Ishmael, never rejected, to the sacred site of Mecca. It is in Mecca where they would personally build the House of God. [13] And Abraham is careful to see to it that Ishmael marries a proper woman who will be worthy of matriarchal status in the genealogical line which will result in the birth of Muhammad, the greatest prophet and the vehicle for God's greatest gift, the Qur'an.

According to Jewish tradition, Ishmael's history became irrelevant to the sacred history of God's people. [14] Sacred history rests in the line of Isaac. But according to Islam, Ishmael is the progenitor of God's greatest prophet who will one day lead his people to establish God's rule on earth. The sacred history of the redemption of humankind through submission to Islam rests entirely in the line of Ishmael.

The Jewish and Islamic versions of the legend of Abraham and his progeny represent a classic example of two religious traditions narrating different and even competing stories about the same paradigmatic characters. This observation is not new. Ever since ancient times, adherents of various religions knew that other religions perceived history and the path to salvation differently, and they often discussed, argued, disputed, and even waged war over their disagreements.

# Competing Religious Views

Each monotheistic religious tradition evolved its own exclusionist defense against the claims of others. Jewish and Christian tradition tended to consider the Islamic claims as mistakes or attempts to distort religious truth in the name of the new temporal power of Islam. Islamic tradition in turn tended to consider Jewish and Christian claims to be the result of tampering with the text of revelation, which originally contained clear prophecies telling of the coming of Muhammad and the rise of Islam. Both biblical and qur'anic scriptures came to be considered by their adherents coeval with Creation. Contradictory claims could not be tolerated. Since the institutions representing monotheistic religions traditionally tend to accept only one truth, only one tradition could possibly be correct. The others are therefore considered either mistaken or purposely distorted.

In recent times, those interested in dialogue between conflicting religious traditions have sought to bridge this gap in a variety of ways. The classic academic approach has tended to analyze the texts of both traditions in order to attempt a determination as to whether one tradition may have "borrowed" from the other, or to try to determine if they both may have evolved out of a common tradition. This methodology breaks down and analyses the various units of each rendition of the legend to try to extract its secrets. Unfortunately, however, the academic approach tends toward reductionism, which has the effect of reducing the power of the legends to merely the sum of simple, even mediocre parts. It tends to ignore the great power—even sublimity—of the literature and the religious truths that legends such as these provide.

A non-reductionist approach to competing religious claims such as these is sorely needed, but the generous efforts of some liberal theologians also seem lacking. Liberal religious thinkers have occasionally constructed theological devices to solve mutually exclusive doctrinal problems such as have been raised here. But these attempts tend to remain unsatisfactory to at least one, and sometimes both parties to the conflict. [15] A third alternative, the view of atheists unsympathetic to religion, suggests that the contradictory claims do nothing more than demonstrate the arbitrariness of religion, showing that religion can only grasp at straws to explain human and natural phenomena and cannot hope to bring reconciliation between religious peoples.

The following approach to competing, even contradictory religious beliefs—such as the example given here with Abraham, Isaac and Ishmael—might serve as a contribution to those interested in the process of interreligious dialogue. This approach requires, first of all, that we be willing to acknowledge that we will never determine the "original" text. Jews have tended to claim that since the biblical canon was established much earlier than that of the Qur'an, the qur'anic stories incorporating biblical characters must represent variants (read "mistakes" or "conscious distortions") of biblical stories.

Muslims, however, claim that the existence of the Qur'an antedates the giving of the Torah on Mt. Sinai because it preceded Creation. As the "Mother of Books," meaning the original or "Urtext" of revelation, the Qur'an is seen as the basis from which all other scriptural revelation is derived. The ancient leaders of Israel were therefore privy to the accurate text of the Torah in which Ishmael's status was indeed primary, but they consciously distorted scripture in order to justify their claim that Judaism would remain God's favored religion. Both Judaism and Islam claim the "original" and therefore "correct" story.

But modern studies in literary theory challenge both views. It has long been evident that stories on biblical themes contemporary with or predating the reception of the biblical tellings have been found in ancient civilizations from Mesopotamia to Egypt. Renderings of many of these legends have probably existed in various forms since time immemorial. It may be argued, therefore, that in the literary sense there never was an "original" telling of the

Abraham story. [16] No religion can justify exclusive owner-ship or the right to an exclusive "Truth" in this regard.

The question of which is the "original" text is a com-pelling one but it is, in the end, the wrong question for people desirous of dialogue. Arguments over which reve-lation came first can never be resolved and are simply counterproductive. They cannot promote dialogue and understanding—only polemics and dispute. Religious leaders must overcome the urge to convince their follow-ing (and themselves) that they have the single absolute truth and move on to the other issues.

## Inter-faith Dialogue

Those engaging in dialogue must be ready to respect the religious impulse of others who pursue different paths to God. This requires an inward faith in the reality of the Divine existing behind the religious quest of humanity. That is, we must be willing, in the words of the great Islamist, Marshall Hodgson, "...to stake our efforts on the hope that something cherished by intelligent and sensitive people over many generations is at least unlikely to be trivial." [17] It more likely contains truths from which we may also learn.

For the religious Jew having grown up believing in the reality of God's covenant with the Jewish people, the Islamic telling of the Abraham-Ishmael story presents a challenge—but not necessarily to one's personal beliefs. It presents a challenge, rather, to one's smugness, to one's general attitude toward other religions. Studying the Islamic approach need not cause us to abandon our beliefs. Rather, it opens our eyes to understand that Muslims, like Jews, see themselves in a special relation-ship with God in their acting out of God's commandments. As we come to understand the depth of this relationship, we learn to respect and value the spirituality and reli-gious impulse of our Muslim cousins even while we recog-nize our different paths.

It must be acknowledged that the call to approach the claims and traditions of another religious system with deep respect and openness may be frightening. If one is willing to accord acceptance of another religion's legitimacy, does it not eventually render even the most fundamental bases of one's own tradition ultimately open to doubt? Perhaps, but this problem seems particularly acute if one accepts a definition of religious truth as absolute, static, and available only to one religious tradition. Modern studies have demonstrated that even some of the most basic truths of the physical universe can no longer be thought of as remaining fixed. Even such stalwart foundations as the nature of matter and time have been found to exhibit relative fluidity. In light of our present knowledge of the physical world, it seems most haughty to claim that in the entirety of the universe God would have allowed religious "Truth" to have been deposited only within one religious tradition. The rabbis themselves could acknowledge that they did not have exclusive ownership to religious truth at the same time that they knew that their path was right for them. They could accept that the pious of all peoples have a share in the world to come,[18] and Rabbi Yohanan could go so far as to say that any person who rejects idolatry could be considered a Jew.[19] Even the biblical rendering of our legend, despite its ultimate rejection of Ishmael, provides him with a divine blessing and acknowledges his twelve sons as princes and founders of twelve tribes,[20] a clear parallel to the twelve sons and twelve tribes of Israel. Abraham's visits to Ishmael in later Jewish tradition further acknowledges that we take the claims of his progeny seriously.[21]

Islam likewise carries traditions that acknowledge the religious claims of others. The Qur'an itself states that Muslim, Jew, Christian, and Sabean—whoever believes in God and the Day of Judgement and has acted righteously—will merit the World to Come.[22] Elsewhere it declares that there should be no compulsion in religion. Whoever rejects evil and believes in God will be saved.[23]

It is not difficult, of course, also to cite the opposite sentiment in both Jewish and Islamic tradition. Although for historical reasons the institutions carrying and perpetuating the authority of the various religious traditions tended toward exclusivism, there have always been valued streams of thought respecting the religious behavior and ideas of other faith traditions, if not always the truth of their religious claims.

This is not to say that religious truth is only relative. God does not change. God is one and is eternal. But human perceptions, understandings of God differ, and our perceptions are affected by many things, including language, culture, technology, and history. Each tradition views God from a different angle and necessarily sees the same reality somewhat differently. No single viewpoint can see all aspects of the Source. As we learn to respect the religiosity and spirituality of the other's tradition at the same time that we affirm the depth and meaning of our own, we need no longer suffer affront nor insecurity when we note the differences between us. We need not try to convince the other to agree with our religious views. That is to say, we need not seek converts. We rather note our differences at the same time that we affirm our commonalities.

When we work together and learn more about one another, even if for limited periods of time, we inevitably learn that some of the negative assumptions we have had about the other are not borne out in fact. We learn to eliminate stereotypes and, subsequently, learn to deal with the important issues in a new and more constructive manner. We need only offer the respect that is due to ancient traditions and religious beliefs, and expect the same in return.

The question of which son of Abraham should be regarded as the one who received God's greatest blessing cannot finally be resolved by us. The more productive question is, can we accept the fact that we have different assumptions and beliefs and still live together? In the world of dialogue, the term "mutual respect" is the key, not "right" or "wrong." With this in mind, we all, the children of Ishmael and the children of Isaac, all of us the children of Abraham, may be able to work together here and abroad in the hopes of building a future beneficial to us all.

1.    This title is based on the Qur'an passage of Sura 3 verse 67: "Abraham was neither a Jew nor a Christian, but was an upright Muslim (Hanifan Musliman), and was not an idol worshipper."

2.    In fact, what the West has often taken for granted as the "Judeo-Christian heritage" would look quite different today without the dramatic influence of systematic thinking as developed in Islam during the Medieval period.

3.    This essay takes the nexus of Jewish and Islamic tradition as its point of departure. Christianity could be included as well but would both delute the poignancy of the Jewish-Islamic interface and require an expanded formulation which is beyond the parameters of this study.

4.    The first mention of this name actually does not appear until 1 Kings 13:19.

5.    Bereshit Rabbah 45:1; Targum Yonatan on Genesis 16:1; Pirkey D'Rabbi Eli'ezer Chapter 26 (61b); Sefer HaYashar (Tel Aviv: Alter-Bergman, 1980): Lekh Lekha, pp. 42, 44; etc.

6.    Genesis 37:25-28, 39:1; Judges 8:22-23; Psalm 83:7. These Ishmaelites were occasionally associated with the Midianites who were also desert peoples and caravan traders (Genesis 37:25 28; Judges 8:22-23).

7.    The qur'anic references are provided below.

8.    The close phonemic relation between the first consonants of each of each word lends support to their view.

9.    The Land of Israel is not referred to as such in Islamic sources, but is generally referred to as Syria *(al-Sha'm)* in Arabic. "The Holy Land" *(al-ard al-muqáddasa*—compare with *ha'eretz ham-quddéshet) is* rarely used, though it undoubtedly derives from Qur'an 5:21 in which Moses urges his people to "...enter the Holy Land which God has assigned to you..."

10.    His death date is 687 CE. Some of the more important sources of the Islamic legend include the encyclopedic Qur'an commentary and universal history of Muhammad b. Jarir al-Tabari (d.923), the Hadith collections of Ibn Hanbal (d.856), al-Bukhari (d.870) and Muslim (d.874), and the popular hagiographies of al-Tha'labi (d.1035) and al-Kisa'i (12th century). For a detailed analysis and translation of the primary Islamic sources, see Reuven Firestone, *Journeys in Holy Lands: The Evolution of the Abraham-Ishmael Legends in Islamic Exegesis* (Albany: State University of New York Press, 1990).

11.    In most renditions of their journey, Abraham is guided to the sacred site of the future Ka'ba by Gabriel or a supernatural angelic being referred to as the Shekhina *(al-sakina).*

12.    The following sequence is the only part of the Islamic story to find a close parallel in Jewish sources. Cf. Pirkey d'Rabbi Eli'ezer 30 (68a-b); Sefer HaYashar, *Vayera* 55-7; Yalqut Shim'oni, Genesis 95, *Vayera* (Jerusalem: Mosad HaRav Kook, 1973) 1:424-25; and the Palestinian Targum on Genesis 21:21.

13.    Islam eventually came to see Ishmael as bound upon the altar at Mecca, thus complementing the biblical portrayal of Isaac bound at Jerusalem. This view, however, became accepted only after the first Islamic century when most Muslims considered Abraham to have laid Isaac on the altar (see Reuven

Firestone, "Abraham's Son as the Intended Sacrifice (Al-Dhabih, Qur'an 37:99-113): Issues in Qur'anic Exegesis," in *Journal of Semitic Studies* 34 (1989), pp. 95-131).

14.    Abraham's journey to Ishmael in the Midrash tends to be understood by modern scholars as an apologetic for Abraham's problematic behavior depicted in Genesis, although Aviva Schussman sees it also as a response to Islam. See her "Abraham's Visits to Ishmael—The Jewish Origin and Orientation" [Hebrew], *Tarbiz* 49 (1980), pp. 325-345; and Joseph Heinemann *Aggadot Ve-Toldoteihen* (Jerusalem, 1974), p. 189ff.

15.    See, for example, the keynote address of Hans Kung at the first meeting of the Harvard Divinity School's Jerome Hall Dialogue Series on October 16, 1984, the responses of Sayyed Hossein Nasr, Veena Das, and Peter Kaufman, and the subsequent discussion, recorded in *Muslim World* 77 (1987), pp. 80-136.

16.    See Jonathan Culler, "Presupposition and Intertextuality," *MLN 91* (1976), pp. 1380-1396; Thais E. Morgan, "Is There an Intertext in this Text? Literary and Interdisciplinary Approaches to Intertextuality," *American Journal of Semiotics* 3 (1985), pp. 1-40; and especially Barbara Herrnstein Smith, "Narrative Versions, Narrative Theories," in W.J.T. Mitchell *On Narrative* (University of Chicago Press, 1981), pp. 209-232.

17.    Marshall G.S. Hodgson, "Two Pre-Modern Muslim Historians: Pitfalls and Opportunities in Presenting Them to Moderns," in John Nef (ed.), *Towards World Community* (The Hague: Dr. W. Junk, 1968), p. 67.

18.    Tosefta, Sanhedrin 13:10.

19.    Megillah 13a. Tosephot (s.v. "kol") lessens the radical nature of Rabbi Yohanan's pronouncement by considering it to refer only to Jews who reject idolatry. It supports the assertion with a reference to a similar discussion in Sanhedrin 93b in which the subjects of discussion were deemed members of the tribe of Judah as opposed to another of the tribes of Israel. Tosephot seems to have had difficulty accepting the generosity of Rabbi Yohanan's words. The context of his statement in Megillah, however, does not entirely clarify his intent.

20.    Genesis 15:16.

21.    See note 12 above.

22.    Qur'an 2:62.

23.    Qur'an 2:256f.

# PHILOSOPHICAL DEVELOPMENTS IN ISLAM AND JUDAISM:

## A MEDIEVAL MODEL FOR THE MODERN WORLD

## Leonard Kravitz

The vagaries of history are such that those who are bitter adversaries at one time may have been amicable partners at another. The history of Jews and Muslims presents such a changing picture. Whatever may be the political problems confronting them at the present time, one should not forget the long history which they have shared. In the past, their reciprocal relationships have been positive and negative in both physical and spiritual terms. Certain religious and cultural developments for each would not have occurred without the existence of the other. One might suggest, for example, that parts of the Koran, the base text of Islam, reflects certain Judaic ideas. [1] Once Islam had developed, spreading first through the Arab peoples and then through others, the relationship between the Jewish people and emerging peoples of Islam would undergo great changes depending upon political as well as religious factors.

Jews and Arabs (and/or non-Arabic Muslims) related as individuals and as adherents of differing and competing religious systems. Those relations, while connected, were not the same. As individuals, they related within the cost-benefit calculus of all peoples, i.e. in terms of power and need. As religionists, they were identified by texts and traditions to which they gave their allegiance and which in turn formed their conceptual worlds. Jews and Muslims were both "People of the Book," albeit different books, books which made conflicting, mutually exclusive claims. Those claims might, and occasionally did, motivate attempts of the one to eliminate the other; however, the presence of need and the absence of power usually precluded such elimination.

Whatever its competition with Jewish groups in its immediate origins, in the next stages of development Islam competed with and conquered many Christian powers in various lands. Having been subservient to Christians, Jews now saw in Islam a welcome successor and a new ally. Those professing Islam would see in the Jews a useful trading community and a reservoir of skills.

Wherever the new conquerors gained dominion, they brought the Koran and the Arabic language. Those Jews who did not already speak Arabic learned the language and subsequently absorbed certain linguistic developments occurring in the Islamic world, such as grammar and poetry. Jews became interested in Hebrew grammar and Hebrew poetry precisely because they lived among people who were interested in Arabic grammar and Arabic poetry.

Grammar and poetry did not reflect the operations of Arabs and Jews qua *religionists*, as adherents of particular faith communities, but rather as *people*—and that is why such cultural elements were transferable from one to the other. Once accepted, grammar could be used to better elucidate a passage of Torah and poetry could be used to compose a hymn to the One Who Gave the Torah. However, it must be stated that the Torah had been studied without the niceties of grammar and Jews had worshipped using only the poetry given in Scripture. Thus Jews could enhance their tradition by something which existed in Islamic culture but which was not specific to Islam.

Philosophy presents a parallel to grammar and poetry in the Islamic and Jewish world in that it was transferable precisely because it was not specific to the one and could enhance the other. In the response of the Arab world and Islam to literature and notions of philosophy, in the intertwining of old beliefs and new ideas, a mold was formed which would shape the model of theological synthesis in Judaism and Christianity when Jews and Christians confronted the same problems of how to respond to old beliefs and new ideas.

The common Arabic language and the positive social interactions of the Islamic and the Jewish communities made possible the acceptance in the Jewish community of the model developed by Muslims. The common language made possible the sharing of books and ideas; the positive relationship allowed for the emulation of philosophical notions. As the intrusion of philosophical ideas touched both communities, first the Islamic and then the Jewish community, the evolution and devolution of various patterns of synthesis occurred first in the Islamic world and then in the Jewish world. So strong is the link between Judaism and Islam in this area, that one must conclude that had there been no Islamic philosophy, there would have been no Jewish philosophy. The great debt that Jewish philosophy owes to its Islamic counterpart becomes clear when examining parallel philosophical developments in Judaism and Islam, particularly in the thought of Saadia Gaon, Judah Halevi, and Moses Maimonides.

Philosophy entered the medieval world in a paradoxical fashion. After originating in Greece to celebrate the work of the mind, its influence spread by reason of the sword, that of Alexander the Great. Though Rome replaced Greece as an imperial power, Greek culture, including philosophy, captivated its new masters and was therefore spread even further. Christianity contributed as another factor in the spread of philosophy. Since the language of the New Testament was Greek, the notion developed that whatever was in Greek was related to Christianity. This association provided the impetus to study Greek and read Greek texts, some of which were philosophical. Monasteries, created by the emerging Christian churches, then provided the labor needed to copy these texts. In time, these Greek manuscripts were not only copied, but also translated into Syriac.

When Islam came upon the scene and swept through the Middle East, texts which had been translated into Syriac were taken up and translated into Arabic, particularly those involving medicine and philosophy. In the same way that Christianity had served as an inadvertent impetus to the spread of philosophy, Islam continued the process. By the nature of things, the texts and ideas of "Greek" thought entered the societal pyramid from the top. After all, the "princes of the faithful," the leaders of the society, were the ones who read this new/old literature and therefore confronted philosophy and its different notions of God, the human person, and the human task— notions which were distant from those presented in the Koran.

The difference between the ideas of Greek philosophy and the Koran generated the first attempt to work out some kind of accommodation between the two worlds. That accommodation was called *kalam*, which is Arabic for "word." Kalam attempted to relate the words of the Koran with the ideas of philosophy. That relation, however ultimately incoherent, attempted to hold on to certain elements of the Islamic tradition which supported the legal structure of society while also retaining other notions which emerged from the philosophical tradition but which, on analysis, would have been destructive to the structure of Islam.

Al Ashari (873-935 CE) of Bagdad, among the first of the Muslims who developed kalam, began a process of theological reflection which expanded beyond the Muslim world. It is not by happenstance that Saadia Gaon (882-942) of Sura (also in Babylonia) wrote a defense of Judaism called *The Book of Beliefs and Opinions*.[2] Following the Islamic model of the kalam, Saadia's work also dealt with unity and justice, first by using creation to establish God's unity and then by arguing for human freedom by claiming that "no one can be held accountable for an act who does not possess freedom of choice."[3] In Saadia, we see a Jewish kalam thinker attempting to relate philosophy to the Torah just as the kalam writers had attempted to synthesize philosophy and the Koran.

When further developments occurred in Islamic world, parallels then appeared in the Jewish world. For example, the person and the thinking of al-Ghazzali (1058-1111) represented a movement away from the kalam approach. In his book *The Incoherence of Philosophy*, al-Ghazzali argued that the synthesis of religion and philosophy attempted by the kalam thinkers had failed and that religious knowledge could come only from Divine Revelation.

Judah Halevi (1085-1141) made a similar argument in his philosophical novella, *The Book of the Kuzari*. [4] Based on a real, if not amazing, event which occurred some four hundred years before, the conversion to Judaism of the entire Khazar people, the book imagines the arguments used to convince their king of the truth of Judaism. The king, troubled by a recurrent dream, invites first a philosopher, next a Christian theologian, and then a Muslim theologian to present their views. The first provides no comfort and the latter two argue as kalam thinkers. Unconvinced, the king then invites a Jewish scholar to present his view. Unlike the Christian and Muslim, the Jew does not argue in the manner of the kalam, beginning with Creation, but he instead starts from the Revelation at Sinai. In the end, religious experience, rather than theological reasoning, proves able to convey religious knowledge.

In response to al Ghazzali, Averroes (1126-1198) presented a more philosophical approach to Islamic religious texts. Born in Cordova, where he served as a judge and a physician, he gained fame within and without the Muslim world as a philosopher and became known as *the* commentator on Aristotle. In his attack upon al Ghazzali, entitled *The Incoherence of the Incoherence*, he argued that philosophy and religion operated on two different levels; the former provided wisdom for a limited group while the latter provided instruction for the majority of people. Therefore, philosophers defended religion, believing "that religious laws are necessary political arts, the principles of which are taken from natural reason and inspiration." [5] Such an approach toward religion, together with his view that the world was not created in a specific moment but was ever created by an eternal deity and hence was eternal, brought the wrath of more conservative theologians upon Averroes. Eventually, he was banished from Cordova and to forced to spend his last days in disgrace in Lucena. He died in Marrakesh.

There was another man born in Cordova who had a similar background as judge and physician and who had a similar impact as a philosopher: Moses Maimonides (1135-1204). Maimonides, whose commentary on the Mishnah and great code of Jewish law, the *Mishneh Torah*, made him the greatest Jewish legalist of his time, wrote a book which caused such controversies that some communities banned one another and Jews killed one another. That book was *The Guide of the Perplexed*. Although, as Maimonides stated in the introduction, the book was directed to the person perplexed by the contrary claims of philosophy and Torah, the book in fact left many of its readers even more perplexed. Its introduction suggested that certain ideas were hidden beneath the surface of Maimonides' words and only certain readers could plumb the depths of Maimonides' meaning. Beginning with a discussion of the word "image," defined as intellect, and ending with a discussion of the word "wisdom," the book suggests some method for the improvement of the intellect and some progression toward wisdom.

For Maimonides, as for Averroes, creation was problematic. Maimonides accepted creation, not because the Torah stated it, but because eternity could not be proven philosophically. Similarly, he accepted revelation, but suggested that it required philosophical preparation. Also, he accepted divine providence, but suggested it depended on the development of the individual human intellect, which required the study of philosophy.

This stress on philosophy presented a problem for many of Maimonides' readers because it made them wonder whether for him was philosophy was more important than Torah. Moreover, Maimonides' view of creation, a crucial theological doctrine, seemed to many to be at best half hearted and at worst to conceal its denial. To require philosophical preparation for prophecy, even were it not sufficient, was to suggest a notion far from the biblical understanding; some of his readers suspected that Maimonides really thought that philosophical preparation *was* sufficient. [6] Similarly, making his view of providence a function of the development of the intellect was to make providence a function of the philosophical preparation required to develop the intellect.

The *Guide* had an explosive impact on the Jewish community as soon as it was translated into Hebrew and thus made available to more readers. The book was attacked and defended; its reading was proscribed and permitted as different communities battled over its meaning. Different commentaries were written to explain it (some sixty commentaries are extant), but to this very day, there is no unanimity as to what Maimonides intended to teach. For many generations and for many Jews, the *Guide* has been the symbol of the permissibility or the impermissibility of philosophy's involvement with Judaism.

As with Saadia and Halevi, one can trace parallels between the views of Maimonides and Averroes. Many of the Jewish philosophers after Maimonides read Averroes and many commentators used Averroes thought to help explain the meaning of the *Guide*. In fact, Averroes was referred to as "one of the theologians." [7]

As these three examples demonstrate, Jewish philosophy reflects the interaction in the Middle Ages of Muslims and Jews as they struggled with new understandings of their world and their faith and attempted to relate what they believed to what they thought. These medieval example should be instructive for contemporary Muslims and Jews.

---

1.    Cf. *Judaism and Islam,* Prolegomenon by Moshe Pearlman, a translation of *Was Hat Mohammed aus den Judenthum aufgenommen* reprint of 1898 edition (New York: Ktav Publishing House, 1970) and Abraham Isaac Katsh,

*Judaism in Islam: Biblical and Talmudic Backgrounds of the Koran and its Commentaries* (New York: NYU Press, *1954).*

2.     Saadia Gaon, *The Book of Beliefs and Opinions,* Samuel Rosenblatt, trans. (New Haven: Yale University Press, 1948).

3.     Saadia Gaon, *The Book of Beliefs and Opinions,* p. 187.

4.     Judah Halevi, *The Book of Kuzari,* Hartwig Hirschfeld, trans. (New York: Pardes Publishing Company, 1946).

5.     Averroes, *Tahafut al-Tahafut (The Incoherence of the Incoherence),* Simon van den Bergh, trans. (Oxford: Oxford Press, 1954), p. 359 (vol. I).

6.     Cf. the commentaries of Shem Tov Efodi to the *Guide* II:32, particularly the statement of Abarbanel: "All the commentators understand from Maimonides' language that he was destroying his own structure and contradicting his own words, since the verses he adduces don't prove his point..." Shem Tov Efodi and Abarbanel are found in *Sefer Moreh Nebuchim,* photoreprint (Jerusalem, 1960).

7.     Moses Narboni, "Introduction," *Commentary on the Guide,* (Om Press, 1946).

# Judeo-Arab Fraternity Rediscovered: A Categorical Imperative for the Twenty-First Century

## Abdelwahab Hechiche

"Wherever you are, some people still investigate under your skin and prayers. Make sure not to flatter their instincts, my son, make sure not to stoop under the multitude! Muslim, Jew, or Christian, they will have to accept you as you are, or to lose you. When the mind of people appears narrow to you, tell yourself that God's earth is vast, and vast are His hands and heart. Never hesitate to move away, far from all the seas, far away from all the borders, from all the homelands, from all the beliefs."

Amin Maalouf, *Leon L'Africain*

"Understanding the other faith is a *conditio sine qua non* of recognition of that faith and cooperation with it. Upon it depends the movement of the mind to drop previous prejudices...Elimination of bias, in turn, is a prerequisite to perception of the other faith as *de jure*, as a legitimate way of relating to God; and these are necessary conditions for the movement of the heart towards appreciation of and willingness to co-operate with the other faith community. Islam's understanding of Judaism occurs on three distinctive levels: It sees members of that faith as humans, as heirs of the Semitic religious tradition, and especially as Jews."

Dr. Ismail R. Al-Faruqi, "Judaism, Zionism and Islam," in *Judaism or Zionism What Difference for the Middle East?*

I have accepted the honor of contributing to this collective effort for two simple reasons: my recent trip to the Middle East with the U.S. Interreligious Committee for Peace in the Middle East enriched me academically and spiritually. My Semitic-Islamic-Maghribi consciousness was tested even when my very Arabic name caused fear and/or suspicion by the Israeli border security personnel. I can say that I found their concern more legitimate and acceptable than the seemingly racial or racist attitudes my Arabic name prompts anytime I am "interviewed" by Western security officers. Yet, while accepting this generous request from my new brother and colleague, Rabbi Gary Bretton-Granatoor, I have to warn the reader of two important points. The first is a weakness: I have no scholarly authority on Jewish-Muslim medieval history. The second is a strength: I have a total confidence in my faith in Judeo-Arab-Islamic fraternity. All the Arab-Israeli wars, the para-military mutual killing, as well as acts of state terror and individual or group acts of terrorism have not stifled either my hope or my optimism for the reawakening of Jewish-Islamic parenthood, a *sine qua non conditio* for the rediscovery of Judeo-Arab fraternity.

# I.   Jews and Arabs: Between *Tradition* and Traditions

When Islam entered the fifteenth century of its history in December, 1979 (*Muharram 1400*; the *Hijra* or Exile of Prophet Mohammed S.A.A.W.S. from Mekka to Medinah opens the Islamic calendar), the Western World experienced a shock. Suddenly, Islam was no longer perceived as a stagnant, archaic religious phenomenon. The Iranian Islamic Revolution startled scholars and statesmen because only a few months earlier, President Jimmy Carter had shared a symbolic "toast" with the Shah-In-Shah, congratulating him for the "stability" of Iran. Whoever learns that one of President Carter's last initiatives was to establish a special fund for the study of Islam can realize the profound political and psychological impact Islam was to have on world affairs. More than the nationalistic and ideological dimensions of the Arab-Israeli conflict, Islam as a religion and as an ideology risked causing more damage than ever in Judeo-Arab, Judeo-Islamic, and Christian-Islamic relations.

## A.  ISLAMIZATION OF IDEOLOGY OR IDEOLOGIZATION OF ISLAM?

Whereas the desire and struggle for a kind of puritanical return to Islamic sources goes back as far as the middle of the nineteenth century, a Western sympathetic interest in Islam is rather recent. What is referred to as the *Salafiyya* was shaped and articulated towards the end of the nineteenth century, under the guidance of thinkers like Jamal Al-Deen Al-Afghani and two of his most important disciples, the Egyptian Mohammed Abduh (1849-1905) and the Syrian Rashid Rida (1865-1935). [1] For Ali Merad, an Algerian Islamicist teaching in Europe, this movement is, above all, the expression of a need and concern for "fidelity to the original community, which is supposed to have experienced the Islamic message in all its plenitude and authenticity." [2] The other new trend is the "ideologization of Islam" which seems to spread all over the Muslim world through the growing visibility or, to use my own neologism, newsibility of "Islamic Fundamentalism."

Having announced the nature of my approach, i.e. my effort to balance my positive subjectivity with a serious professional effort at a scientific analysis, I elect to pay more attention to those Muslim and non-Muslims who have been trying to return to the "sources" for a better and more constructive understanding of the Revelation not only to Prophet Mohammed, but also to His predecessors, all the Prophets named in the Holy Qur'an, and in particular, Moussa or Moses, and Issa or Jesus, may the Almighty "exalt" them, to use Maimonides' way of referring to the Prophets of his own faith.

## B. THE TRADITION OF JUDEO-ARABIC-ISLAMIC CO-EXISTENCE

Although I happen to have found some serious contradictions in Professor Bernard Lewis' comments on "Orientalism" in the context of the Cold War, [3] his views on Islam in its relationship with the "People of the Book," are very pertinently substantiated with quotations from the Qur'an and corroborated by other scholarly research. After an emphasis on Islam's followers as *"Umma dun Al-nas,* a people or community distinct from the rest of mankind,"* Professor Lewis reminds us of the more important rejection of paganism by Islam. Hence, "inevitably, the struggle against paganism brought Islam closer to Judaism and Christianity, seen, if not as allies, then as kindred faiths opposed to a common adversary." [4] More importantly, Professor Lewis stresses the emerging "sense of kinship, at least in later times, in the consciousness of all three communities." With the assistance of the Qur'an and later commentators and exegetes, Professor Lewis seems very confident that one can speak of "religious pluralism, and even of coexistence" in Islam:

> For most of the Middle Ages the Jews of Islam comprised the greater and more active part of the Jewish people. The Jews who lived in Christian countries, that is in Europe, were a minority, and a relatively unimportant one at that. With few exceptions, whatever was creative and significant in Jewish life happened in Islamic lands. [5]

It is in that Tradition that one should find the source of the renewal of Judeo-Arab-Islamic relations—if not fraternal relations, at least a reason for a "good neighborhood policy." My colleague, Professor Ali Merad, offers one of the most eloquent *mise au point* regarding the nuances within and between the Islamic Tradition and Islamic traditions: "The numerous Qur'anic references focused on the concept *Deen* (religion?), place the latter in a semantic field where the three following notions are articulated: faith, cult, and spiritual tradition, in this case the

Abrahamic tradition, which is supposed to have been periodically reactualized through the succession of the prophets."

It is exactly the same idea we heard from the revered Mufti of Syria during our recent peace mission to the Middle East. To those who might have been or still are threatened by the challenge of a third monotheistic religion, Ali Merad offers the most reassuring interfaith interpretation: "If Islam appears specifically in this semantic field, it is not in the name of a new values system in rupture with the previous tradition, but as the reaffirmation of the latter, in a necessarily new linguistic and cultural expression." Ali Merad uses the Qur'an to support this reassuring view for the followers of the three Peoples of the Book: "To each prophet we assigned nothing but a teaching mission for his people in his own language" (Qur'an, XIV,4). [6]

## II. Ethnicity, Religion, and Nationalism in Judeo-Arab Relations

### A. NORTH AFRICAN JEWS: BETWEEN ARAB NATIONALISM AND ZIONISM

Beyond my Islamic conviction regarding my brotherhood with Jews and Christians, it is my North African-Tunisian experience that adds tremendously to my consciousness of my Semitic-Maghribi identity. I dare say that what was recognized by the Foundation de la Vocation as my commitment to "Judeo-Arab fraternity and Arab-Israel rapprochement" in Paris in 1965 became my professional academic interest and an existential obsession. But in 1983, thanks to the NEH Summer Fellowship at the Center for Middle Eastern Studies of Harvard University, I undertook my first "scientific" investigation of the potential and actual roles of North African Jews in Arab-Israeli relations. [7] A. Ibn Khaldun's work opened new horizons for my intellect and for my human perceptions of ethnonational and ethnoreligious conflicts. I keep in mind and in my heart the quintessence of the Islamic attitude regarding *Ahl Al-Kitab* (The People of the Book), which is contained in the phrase *"Lakum deenukum wa lee deenee"* (To you, your religion, and to me, my religion!). My ongoing effort is to reach a synthesis of my subjective attitude and my academic strife to acquire some authority to prove the existence of positive, actual, and potential roles for the Sephardim in the area of trust-building between the State of Israel and the whole Arab world. My view is that with the rediscovery of past fraternity, Jews and Arabs (Christians and Muslims) would make the "unthinkable" [8] Palestinian State not only possible, but also quite desirable.

## B. THE COLONIAL FACTOR IN JUDEO-ARAB RELATIONS

Using the scholarly authority of North African Jews such as Andre Chouraqui, David Corcos and others, Marion Woolfson makes an important distinction between experiences of Jews in the east and west:

> At the present time, many Westerners make the mistake of comparing countries in the Middle East with those of the West and expecting identical social conditions, in spite of the fact that there is no logical basis for comparison between the two areas as the rate of progress and standards are entirely different. Similarly, the same criteria are applied to the past, although the history of the Jews of the Middle East and North Africa has been basically different from that of Western Jews; the Western Jew fails to realize this because he is inclined to interpret the problem of Eastern Jewry in the light of his own quite different historical experience and see them through the eye of a Westerner. Until the end of the ghetto era, Western Jews belonged to self-contained groups with their own customs and traditions, quite separate from the local non-Jews. In the Middle East, however, the Jews have always belonged to the ethnic society. Jewish myths, legends, rites and superstition were all part of Eastern tradition...As people

became more and more conscious that they were members of nation-states, so they increasingly resented the communal sense of identity of the Jews who lived among them, but this outlook was totally absent in the East until nationalism spread in modern times. [9]

For Chouraqui, the occasional violence against Jews was, in great part, caused by "the abject misery in which feudalism had plunged the entire population of the region." This is exactly my main argument against those who, sincerely or not, believed and tried to make the world believe that "Jews were persecuted" in Arab-Islamic lands. It is certainly true that Jews did not experience or benefit from democratic values in their Arab countries of origin. Who did? Most of those countries were under direct or indirect European colonialism. As a matter of fact, a closer look into the French penetration of North Africa, or that of Great Britain in the Mashrek, will reveal to us a Machiavellian policy of "divide and rule" which contributed to the dilemma to be faced by the Jewish communities: Should they remain on the side of conservative traditionalism or embrace the promises offered by European modernity through education in science and technology?

The chronological French colonial impact on North Africa explains very easily the quantitative and qualitative reaction of the Jewish communities in Algeria (since 1830), in Tunisia (since 1881-82), and in Morocco, where resistance to France lasted until 1912. Quoting David Corcos and Georges Vajda, Chouraqui gives us the ultimate image of what many had already called the "Judaeo-Islamic Symbiosis":

In the Middle Ages, relations between Jews and Muslims, in Spain and in the Maghreb, were so interwoven that some Jews would not hesitate to pray in mosques, mixed with Muslims. When the latter pronounced their *Shahada*, the Jews proclaimed the *Shema Israel*, without any fear that

Jewish particularism would hurt Islamic prose-
lytism. [10]

When we move to the more populist religious practices,
we find an equal Judeo-Arab symbiosis in superstition,
magic, and the cult of saints. Professor Issaachar Ben
Ami's exhaustive study of Moroccan saints is quite revealing. Out of six hundred and fifty two saints, of unequal
importance, one hundred and twenty six are venerated by
Jews and Muslims alike. [11] This is certainly the real cause
of the cultural shock experienced by Sephardim and
Ashkenazim during their "reunion" in their "Promised
Land." The Tunisian Jewish writer and scholar, Albert
Memmi, who contributed to the Tunisian nationalist
struggle against colonialism, did not spare the Arab world
of some of his sharpest criticism; but he never denied his
"Arabness." On the contrary, when Sephardic Jews, especially those of North Africa, were experiencing a quasi
racial discrimination (as paradoxical as this might sound),
Albert Memmi took his most lethal weapon, his pen, to
write to the leaders of Israel and protest such a humilia-
tion for his Arab Jewish brethren.

I cannot finish this part of the essay without returning
to a more positive aspect of the Judeo-Arab symbiosis.
This concerns the language used by both Jews and
Muslims of Arab lands: classical Arabic and local dialects.
Andre Chouraqui considers the above mentioned traits of
the Judeo-Arab tradition less significant than the following:

> For eight centuries, the greatest synagogue theolo-
> gians wrote their principal works in the sacred lan-
> guage of Islam, Arabic. This linguistic connivance is
> the manifest sign of a unique cultural and political
> connivance. On the other hand, never did any Jew
> think of writing in Latin in the midst of Medieval
> Christianity. [12]

Another source, Prime Minister David Ben Gurion,
confirms Chouraqui's point. In the early fifties, Ben
Gurion used to spend his lunch time to learning Arabic in
order to read Maimonides' work in its original version. [13]

# III. Shalom, Pax, Peace, Salaam: Theory and Practice?

## A. INTELLECT AND FAITH IN JUDEO-ISLAMIC THOUGHT

In his acceptance speech for the 1986 Nobel Peace Prize, Elie Wiesel declared:

> Sometimes we must interfere. When human lives are endangered, when human dignity is in jeopardy, national borders and sensitivities become irrelevant. Wherever men or women are persecuted because of their race, religion, or political views, that place must—at that moment—become the center of the universe. [14]

There is no doubt that as we approach the twenty-first century, our human conditions seems to be more miserable than ever. This is all the more tragic as we are led to believe that the end of the Cold War is opening the gate for a New International Order. Professor Phillip E. Hammond and Ninian Smart were perceptive enough in their joint preparation for the 1986 NEH Seminar on "Religion and Nationalism: The Dilemma of Citizenship" to write:

> In order to understand our world, it is crucial to understand that it is pluralistic, and that religious pluralism contributes fundamentally to the diversity of nations. The world is not, contrary to some opinions, growing secular. Religion is not disappearing, though it is certainly undergoing a change, which thus alters the relation between it and nationalism. Events in Poland, Iran, Northern Ireland...for example, cannot be understood without a consideration of the religious situations in these countries, situations embedded in movements towards political rights, cultural identity, and national autonomy. Even the Moral Majority, we would argue, is not merely a religious phenomenon in the narrow sense; it is one very significant factor in the battle over American culture.

More than anywhere else, "Arab Jews" and "Israeli Arabs" have dialectically suffered from and/or contributed to the dilemma of citizenship, under the respective pressures of Zionism and Arab nationalism. Twice between 1984 and August, 1986 King Hassan II of Morocco startled the world by hosting a Jewish Congress with members of the Knesset of Moroccan origin and then with Prime Minister Shimon Peres. In April 1986, *The Jerusalem Post* quoted a Muslim Israeli, Dr. Sami Ma'ari, a psychologist, who affirmed that "the hatred of Arabs that Israelis of Middle Eastern origin are generally assumed to feel is only skin-deep, and has no ideological basis." Another optimistic view comes from Professor Charles Hoffman who maintains: "The conventional ways of examining the attitudes of Sephardim to Arabs and the prospects of peace have held up a distorting mirror to Sephardic culture and history."[15]

Already in 1979, Professor Emmanuel Gutman had perceived that "religion was playing a many-faceted and ambiguous role in the integrative process in the Israeli Jewish community." He also added that religion "was endowed with a dual contradictory function: a source of disaffection, dissent and conflict on one hand" and "to the extent that it provides a common sentiment, it preserves a common attachment and loyalties and thus serves as a fusionary element." This is certainly true of all Jewish communities as minorities from the shores of Morocco to China. But I find it difficult to share Professor Gutman's confident assertion that "Judaism...contrary to many other religions, hardly ever departed from its path as a mono-ethnic religion, and this has strengthened ethno-national coherence among Jews, both in practice and in purpose." On the other hand, Professor Gutman's view holds only when the Jews have a minority status. Reflecting on the Ottoman rule, he writes:

> The Jewish community presented the least difficulty to the Ottomands in their reorganization of the non-Muslim religious groups, because among the Jews, ethnicity, religion, and community coincided. Thus

the *millet* established with its own *hahambashi* (chief rabbi) continuing in authority, an arrangement that seems to have been highly unusual.

In fact, according to Kemal Karpat: "The Jewish community was from the start close to the apparent Ottoman ideal of the synthesis of ethnicity, religion, and community that was to be the building material of its political edifice." [16] In September 1992, the Sephardim of Turkey celebrated 500 good years. [17]

## B. ETHNICITY IN MODERN ARAB-ISRAELI RELATIONS

### 1. A Conceptual Approach

According to Harold R. Isaacs: "An individual belongs to his basic group in the deepest and most literal sense that he is not alone...He is not only not alone, but as long as he chooses to remain in it, he cannot be denied or rejected. It is an identity that no one can take away from him." This prompts an idea that may have become a cliche, but that nonetheless remains valid. As Isaacs asserts: "You can take the Palestinians out of Palestine, but you cannot take Palestine out of the Palestinians." And, very frankly, when I realized that I admired the Jews for having remembered and dreamt "Next year in Jerusalem" for two thousand years, I could not help wondering how one could expect the Palestinians to forget after only less than fifty years.

In their introduction to *Ethnicity*, Nathan Glazier and Daniel Moynihan simply, but so accurately, suggest: "A new word reflects a new reality and a new usage reflects a change in that reality." They present the new word as "ethnicity" and the new usage as the steady expansion of the term "ethnic group from minority and from marginal sub-groups at the edges of society—groups expected to assimilate, to disappear, to continue as survivors, exotic or troublesome—to major elements of society." The most striking fact from such studies is their corroboration by the most recent events in major regions of the world such as in African, South Asia, and the heart of Europe.

R. S. McLaurin defines a minority as "a body of persons

with a sense of cohesion who, taken together, constitute less than one half of the population of an entity." He also notes that "minorities may, theoretically, include political factions, social or economic groups, religious communities, either sex or age groups, occupational groups, language or racial groups." [18] In trying to present minorities as a component of political power, McLaurin suggests that an effective socialization can be the source of "strength to minority identity in these groups" and "the backbone of resistance to assimilation." For the sake of clarity, I would like to use a long quotation from McLaurin's introduction to *Minorities and Politics in the Middle East:* [19]

> Cohesive minorities can pose major problems for governments of countries in which the political order itself, and the regime as well, do not possess established legitimacy. Minorities' group loyalties are often more real than state loyalty, and, consequently, decisions at the state level are frequently made with a view to retaining these groups' conditional allegiance. State policy is, in effect, held hostage to minority will. Where there are several of such groups within a single policy, state nationalism may be a myth—a concept felt by no major portion of the populace. It is true that when one refers to the abundant literature supporting the concept of *integrative modernization*, it becomes natural that the existence of minority groups and its implicit power can be seen as anomalous, anachronistic, dysfunctional, and most important, evanescent. [20]

## 2. The Israeli Case — Arab Jews and Israeli Arabs: What Role for Shalom-Salaam?

I use Glazier and Moynihan's observation (*Beyond the Melting Pot*) regarding the emergence of ethnic consciousness at a time when ethnic groups are supposed to disappear. [21] The myth of Arab Unity, reinforced by the sentiment of Islamic "brotherhood" (not to confuse this with the *Muslim Brotherhood* of Hassan Al-Banna in Egypt), unquestionably has contributed to the survival of a cultural, political, and religious identity in Arab-Islamic societies where Jews played a major role in the history of those countries, including national struggles against colonialism. Against such a background, I still see North African Jews as "a large, well defined diaspora which, in some respects, is different from Jewish groups generally, even from those of the Muslim East or Mashrek, in particular." [22] On the other hand, like the myth of a united Arab world, or, even that of *Dar-Al-Islam*, it seems to me that the miraculous re-birth of the Jewish state has also been wrapped by a multi-dimensional myth.

In his major work, *Israeli Society*, N. S. Eisenstadt explains the dynamics of Israeli internal policy, in particular when the new state had to fill various gaps left by the Mandatory Power, the Arabs who fled, and even the Yishuv. Because of the pressure of limited space, I shall retain some of the most pertinent points of Eisenstadt's analysis. The state saw an increase in the claims made by various groups for allocation of resources, which changed the basis of solidarity within the Yishuv. The significant increase of the Israeli population was to become the second major cause of social change. In that process, both quantitavely and qualitatively, the Sephardim—especially North Africans—began to take a new importance in the evolution of Israeli society which, willy-nilly, will make them one of the major determinants of Israel's orientation toward peace or war in the Middle East. [23] Let's not forget that the lack of harmony, to say the least, in the Muslim world is comparable to the division of the Jewish world that was narrowly avoided when the Kenesset put aside the "Who is a Jew" issue.

To such fundamental conceptual studies, one could add those of Joseph Rotschild and Walker Connor regarding ethnopolitics and ethnonationalism. However, having become aware that "peace-loving" is in itself a form of faith, my ongoing effort to study Jewish-Arab relations goes beyond the negative projection that "ethnic divisions will persist into the future and that they bode ill for the long-term stability of the Israeli political system, and, derivatively, the Israeli ability to deal effectively with her

Arab neighbors." [24] R. Bar Yosef expresses an even greater fear: Ethnic groups may turn into pressure groups that could transform "the Knesset into a forum of struggling national minorities with no other political vision other than the preservation and fostering of their own ethnic interest." These views raise the question: Where does all this lead us when contemplating Judeo-Christian-Arab-Islamic relations in America?

## IV. A New Opportunity for Judeo-Arab Fraternity in the USA

It seems to me that certain societal phenoma observed by Alexis de Tocqueville are still identifiable with the more recent waves of immigrants. Walt Whitman's America has transcended its continentality to reach its truly universal dimension. This seemingly transnational, transconfessional, and transethnic vocation of the "Land of Opportunity" may be a divine gift for humankind not only to live happily ever after, but to use this land for reconciliation. Many pairs of former enemies or adversaries have found themselves face to face in America: Germans and French, Greeks and Turks, etc. Although the Jews are among some of the strongest and oldest communities, their heterogeneity is reflective of all European immigrants (from the Atlantic to the Urals). As for the Arabs, their presence in America began with Christian Arabs, which may explain the delay in the manifestation of Arab Muslim culture and religion in North America. But the real new kid on the block is the Sephardic community, considered a "minority-within-a-minority." [25]

This represents an additional reason for Jews and Arabs (Christians and Muslims) to work together for the revival of past fraternal interreligious and inter-cultural coexistence. If indeed the United States government is to be the only diplomatic channel for Arab-Israeli-Palestinian peace-making, I cannot imagine any Jewish or Arab people of good will not being committed to a fraternal inter-communal relationship. The permanent goal of such a relationship should be to contribute to peace in the Middle East and to peace between Jews, Christians, and Muslims wherever they live.

1.    The *Salafiyyah* movement, through its publication *Al Manar,* sought to restate classical doctrines in order to bring about Islamic political, legal, and intellectual reform. See *Voices of Resurgent Islam,* ed. J. Esposito (Oxford, 1983), 6.

2.    Ali Merad, *L'Islam A l'Horizon* 2000 (XVe Siecle de l'Hegire) in *Revue Tiers-Monde,* Tome XXIII, No. 92 (Octobre-Decembre 1982), 758.

3.    Abdelwahab Hechiche, Les Etudes Arabes, Islamiques, Mediterraneennes et Inter-culturelles aux Etats-Unis," in *Etudes Internationales,* Tunis, Spring 1988.

4.    Bernard Lewis, *The Jews of Islam* (Princetion: Princeton University Press, 1984), 12.

5.    Bernard Lewis, "The Judaeo-Islamic Tradition," in *The Jews of Islam,* 67. I believe that these words were first written by S.D. Goitein who receives more credit in note 2 of ch. 2, p. 203.

6.    Ali Merad, "Le Message Originel," in *L'Islam A L'Horizon 2000, 762.*

7.    The seminar dealt with "Muslim Minorities in the Middle East and in the Soviet Union," under the co-directorship of Drs. E. Naby and R. Frye. Although my research project focused on the Berbers, I managed to undertake preliminary research about North African Jews because of their pre-Arab and pre-Islamic presence in the Maghrib.

8.    Walid Khalidi, "Thinking the Unthinkable: A Palestinian State," in *Foreign Affairs* (July 1978), 695-713.

9.    Marion Woolfson, *Prophets in Babylon: Jews in the Arab World* (Faber, 1980), 39.

10.    Andre Chouraqui, "L'Eclatement D'Une Cite," in *Les Juifs D 'Afrique du Nord,* 354-360.

11.    Agnes Bensiman, *Hassan Il Et Les Juifs,* Editions Du Seuil (Paris, 1991), 23.

12.    Chouraqui, 356.

13.    Thanks to a *Maghreb Review* Conference on Islam in the Maghreb, held at Cambridge University in the mid eighties when the Library organized a special exhibit of Arabic texts of Medieval Islam. It was the first time that I had the moving privilege of seeing some of Maimonides' works and even some prescriptions by Jewish doctors in Alexandria or Cairo.

14.    Elie Wiesel, Acceptance Speech, 1986 Nobel Peace Prize, Oslo.

15.    Charles Hoffman, "How Sephardim Feel About Arabs?", *The Jerusalem Post,* November 12, 1986.

16.    Kemal Karpat, "The Ottoman Ethnic and Confessional Legacy in the Middle East," in *Ethnicity, Pluralism, and the State in the Middle East,* ed. Milton J. Esman and Itamar Rabinovich (Cornell University Press, 1988).

17.    Alan Cowell, "Sephardim Celebrate 500 Good Years," *The New York Times International,* September 14, 1992, p. A4.

18.    R. D. McLaurin, "Minorities and Politics in the Middle East: An

Introduction," in *The Political Role of Minority Groups in the Middle East,* ed. R.D. McLaurin (New York: Praeger, 1979), 4.

19.    See note 16.

20.    Ibid.

21.    N. Glazier and P. D. Moynihan, *Beyond The Melting Pot: The Negroes, Puerto-Ricans, Jews, Italians and Irish of New* York (Cambridge: M.I.T. Press, 1970).

22.    H. Z. Hirsbergg, "From Antiquity to the Sixteenth Century," in *A History of the Jews in North Africa,* Vol. I (Leiden: E.J. Brill, 1981).

23.    Eisenstadt's Tables of Ethnic-Demographic Data are to be compared with Shlomo Deshen's *Immigrant Voters in Israel,* 65-66.

24.    Lee E. Dutter, "Eastern and Western Jews, Ethnic Divisions in Israeli Society, in *The Middle East Journal* (Summer 1977), 451. This author's bibliography is rich in sources on ethnicity.

25.    Abraham D. Lavender has paid serious attention to the demographic and cultural importance of the new American Sephardic Jews by studying their "attempts at ethnic revival" and the potential "sociological benefits from the study of the Sephardim." Abraham D. Lavender, "The Sephardic Revival in the United States: A Case of Ethnic Revival in a Minority-Within a Minority," in *The Journal of Ethnic Studies,* 1975, 3 (3), 21-31.

**Program #1**

# INTRODUCTION:
# THE JOURNEY BEGINS

**Overview:**

This program is designed to introduce the participants to one another and to the structure of this eight-session dialogue. Moving from the realm of the theoretical to the personal, the program begins by examining some of the notions of interreligious dialogue that guide this project and ends with the participants sharing their own experiences and ideas. Central to this program is the image of dialogue as a journey. In the midst of travelling on separate paths, the opportunity for Jewish-Muslim dialogue allows individual Muslims and Jews to meet, establish relationships, and together venture forth on a vital course of education, enrichment, and support.

**Outline:**

I.   Welcome: Introduction and General Overview
II.  Insights Guiding Our Path: Ideas on Interreligious Dialogue
III. Charting Our Journeys: Who Are We & What Brings Us Here?
IV.  Looking Ahead: Preparation for Program #2
V.   Sanctifying the Journey

**Procedure:**

**I.   Welcome: Introduction and General Overview**

1.   Welcome participants.

2.   Introduce facilitators.

3.  Distribute a schedule listing the topic, date, and location of each session and give an overview of the dialogue.

## II. Insights Guiding Our Path: Ideas on Interreligious Dialogue

*Introductory Remarks:* This section of the program seeks to acquaint the participants with the main principles that undergird this eight-session dialogue. In addition, the quotations are designed to spark a more general discussion about the potential of interreligious dialogue and to allow the participants to express their own expectations and motivations for engaging in Jewish-Muslim dialogue. The lay-out of the *On Dialogue* hand-out provides room for the facilitators to supplement the list of statements by inserting quotations from other sources or adding their own words.

1.  Distribute *On Dialogue* and introduce this section of the program.

2.  One by one, read and discuss the quotations (as a guide, the annotated hand-out highlights several points drawn from the quotations). Suggested questioning sequence for each statement:

    a. How would you rephrase this statement in your own words?

    b. In what ways might this notion shape the structure or content of interreligious dialogue?

3.  Synthesize the quotations and comments.

    a. Thinking about your own expectations and motivations for engaging in Jewish-Muslim dialogue, what statement would you add to this list?

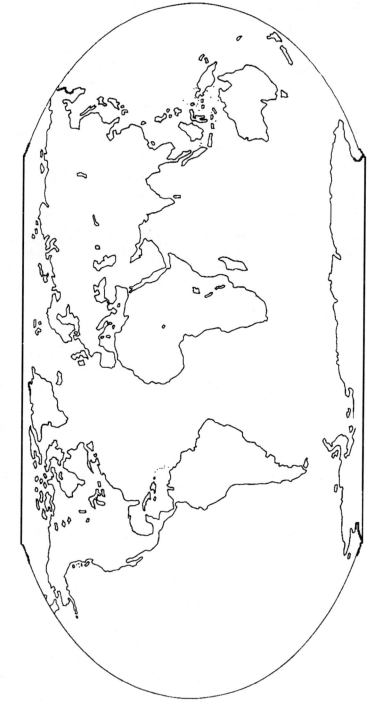

**Charting Our Journeys**

## III. Charting Our Journeys: Who Are We & What Brings Us Here?

*Introductory Remarks:* The third part of this program provides an opportunity for the participants to introduce themselves and tell a bit about their personal backgrounds. The participants will be given a map and asked to chart the path that brought them to their present involvement in Jewish-Muslim dialogue. As the participants describe their personal travels, they will hopefully begin to recognize some of the common experiences and values shared by American Muslims and Jews.

1. Pass out maps and pens.

2. Instruct the participants to sketch the path which has brought them to their present involvement in Jewish-Muslim dialogue.

   a. This activity is intentionally open, allowing the participants to interpret the project as fits their background or interests. For example, some may trace their physical movement from city to city, while others may chart important points in their religious development or mark their lives in other ways.

3. After the participants have finished, ask them to introduce themselves and briefly explain their maps.

## IV. Looking Ahead: Preparation for Program #2

1. In preparation for the next session, ask the participants to read Reuven Firestone's article, "Abraham: The First Jew or the First Muslim? Text, Tradition, and 'Truth' in Interreligious Dialogue."

## V. Sanctifying the Journey

*Introductory Remarks:* As explained above, dialogue brings Jews and Muslims together on a common path of discovery, understanding, and friendship. The program concludes with the sanctification of this journey through prayer.

1. Muslims: Recite "An Islamic Prayer for a Journey."
2. Jews: Recite *"Tefillat Ha-derech*: A Jewish Prayer for a Journey."
3. Concluding remarks by facilitators.

**Materials:**
1. Participants will need a copy of each hand-out:
    a. *Dialogue Overview* (schedule listing the topic, date, and location of each session)
    b. *On Dialogue* (if desired, add quotations or phrases to the hand-out)
    c. *Charting Our Journeys*
    d. *Sanctifying the Journey of Dialogue*
2. Colored marking pens
3. Name tags

# ON DIALOGUE (Annotated Version)

1. "HOW TRUE IT IS THAT ONE UNDERSTANDS A FAITH BETTER BY KNOWING ITS BELIEVERS RATHER THAN READING ITS THEORETICIANS."

**Comments:**

This statement helps us understand that Jews and Muslims can best learn about Islam and Judaism through dialogue, rather than simply reading books or attending lectures on "Islamic Beliefs" or "Jewish Practice." Instead, we have much to teach about our religious traditions by telling one another about our own religious lives. Recognizing each other not as official representatives of our entire religious traditions, but as individuals who express our religious identities in our unique ways, a seemingly abstract or distant tradition can come alive in a personal, understandable way.

**Source:**

Eugene B. Borowitz, "On Theological Dialogue with Christians," *Exploring Jewish Ethics* (Detroit: Wayne State University Press, 1990), 394.

2. "PERHAPS THE MOST IMPORTANT LESSON WE HAVE LEARNED ABOUT INTERPERSONAL AND INTERRELIGIOUS DIALOGUE IN RECENT YEARS IS THAT WE MUST MAKE A DETER-MINED EFFORT TO GET TO KNOW PEOPLE AS THEY ARE, NOT AS WE, FOR WHATEVER REA-SON, WOULD HAVE THEM BE."

**Comments:**

This quotation urges us to put aside stereotypes and look at one another through a lens untainted by stereo-types and expectations. If dialogue is to be truly meaning-ful and transformative, we must demonstrate an ablity to listen well and an openness to letting others surprise us, challenge us, and teach us.

**Source:**

Eugene B. Borowitz, *Contemporary Christologies* (New York: Paulist Press, 1980), 7.

3. "THE FIRST STEP TOWARD UNDERSTANDING SOMETHING ALIEN IS THE DISCOVERY OF SOME COMMON ELEMENT SHARED BY BOTH YOU AND THE OTHER."

**Comments:**

This comment emphasizes the importance of beginning dialogue with topics which will foster understanding and sensitivity.

**Source:**

Jay Kinney, "Islam as Other" (Chicago: The Institute of Islamic Information and Education).

4. "ONLY BY DIRECTLY CONFRONTING OUR DEEP-EST DIFFERENCES CAN WE COME TO KNOW ONE ANOTHER FULLY. WE ARE WHO WE ARE AS MUCH BY OUR DIVERGENCE FROM ONE ANOTHER AS BY OUR SIMILARITY. PARADOXI-CAL AS IT SOUNDS, I DO NOT THINK WE PROP-ERLY COMPREHEND OUR OWN RELIGION UNTIL WE SEE IT IN ITS DISTINCTIVE DIFFER-ENCE FROM OTHER HUMAN FAITHS."

**Comments:**

This citation moves beyond the previous quotation, reminding us that interreligious dialogue is not only a process of recognizing and celebrating similarities, but also of confronting and grappling with differences. Although shared experiences and values provide a founda-tion for building comradery and understanding, we must be willing to move beyond the niceties of our commonali-ties and able to face the harder task of dealing with our differences. In doing so, we will better understand other religious traditions and our own as well.

**Source:**

Eugene B. Borowitz, *Contemporary Christologies* (New York: Paulist Press, 1980), 20.

5.  "SENSITIVITY AND COMMUNICATION GROW OUT OF A MUTUAL NEED TO UNDERSTAND AND TO BE UNDERSTOOD."

**Comments:**

This statement highlights some of the most important elements of interreligious dialogue: sensitivity to other's beliefs and practices, openness to sharing one's own faith, and a capacity to listen to others with respect and to acknowledge the integrity and divinity of their faith.

**Source:**

Michael A. Signer, *"Communitas et Universitas:* From Theory to Practice in Judaeo-Christian Studies," in *When Jews and Christians Meet*, ed. Jakob J. Petuchowski (New York: State University of New York Press), 74.

# ON DIALOGUE

1. "HOW TRUE IT IS THAT ONE UNDERSTANDS A FAITH BETTER BY KNOWING ITS BELIEVERS RATHER THAN READING ITS THEORETICIANS."

2. "PERHAPS THE MOST IMPORTANT LESSON WE HAVE LEARNED ABOUT INTERPERSONAL AND INTERRELIGIOUS DIALOGUE IN RECENT YEARS IS THAT WE MUST MAKE A DETERMINED EFFORT TO GET TO KNOW PEOPLE AS THEY ARE, NOT AS WE, FOR WHATEVER REASON, WOULD HAVE THEM BE."

3. "THE FIRST STEP TOWARD UNDERSTANDING SOMETHING ALIEN IS THE DISCOVERY OF SOME COMMON ELEMENT SHARED BY BOTH YOU AND THE OTHER."

4. "ONLY BY DIRECTLY CONFRONTING OUR DEEPEST DIFFERENCES CAN WE COME TO KNOW ONE ANOTHER FULLY. WE ARE WHO WE ARE AS MUCH BY OUR DIVERGENCE FROM ONE ANOTHER AS BY OUR SIMILARITY. PARADOXICAL AS IT SOUNDS, I DO NOT THINK WE PROPERLY COMPREHEND OUR OWN RELIGION UNTIL WE SEE IT IN ITS DISTINCTIVE DIFFERENCE FROM OTHER HUMAN FAITHS."

5. "SENSITIVITY AND COMMUNICATION GROW OUT OF A MUTUAL NEED TO UNDERSTAND AND TO BE UNDERSTOOD."

# SANCTIFYING THE JOURNEY

**An Islamic Prayer for a Journey**

In the name of Allah,
whether it move or be at rest;
for my Lord is, be sure, oft-forgiving and Most Merciful:
When so seated, you should remember
the kind favor of your Lord and say:
Glory to Allah who has subjected these to our use,
for we would never be able to act
except by the help of Allah.
And to our Lord,
surely must we turn back.
O my Lord, You are my companion on my journey,
and the successor in my family, children, and prosperity.
O my Lord, I seek refuge in You
against the devil and all difficulties
that may face me on my trip.
O, Allah, I pray to You to make me safe,
and to afford safety to my family
during my absence.
Amin.

*Tefillat Ha-derech:* **A Jewish Prayer for a Journey**

May it be Your will,
Eternal our God and God of our ancestors,
to guide us in peace and sustain us in peace,
to lead us to our desired destination in health and joy
and to bring us home in peace.
Save us from every enemy and disaster on the way
and from all calamities that threaten the world.
Bestow blessing upon the work of our hands,
that we may find grace, love, and companionship
in Your sight and in the sight of all who see us.
Hear our pleas,
for You are a God who listens to our prayers and pleas.
Praised are You, who listens to prayer.

# Program #2

# ABRAHAM: SHARED ANCESTORS AND SACRED TEXTS

## Overview:

This program looks at Abraham and his family from numerous vantage points. After watching the video *Abraham and His Children*, the remainder of the program focuses on Jewish and Islamic views of a specific chapter in Abraham's life: the expulsion of Hagar and Ishmael. The program also provides a brief introduction to the content and development of Jewish and Islamic sacred literature. The session concludes with the difficult questions: How can members of different faiths best deal with conflicting religious beliefs?

## Outline:

I.   Video: *Abraham and His Children*

II.  Text Study: Abraham, Hagar, and Ishmael in Judaism and Islam

III. Searching for Answers: Approaches to Conflicting Traditions

IV.  Looking Ahead: Preparation for Program #3

## Procedure:

### I.   Video: *Abraham and His Children*

*Introductory Remarks*: This twenty-five minute video features Jewish, Muslim, and Christian scholars, along with their students and colleagues, discussing the figure of Abraham and his significance for each faith. The film explores the covenant tradition, the sacrifice of Isaac, and Abraham's journey. Besides demonstrating the similarities and differences in each faith's understanding of our common ancestor, the film provides a window onto the world of the synagogue and the mosque.

1. Watch video.

## II. Text Study: Abraham, Hagar, and Ishmael in Judaism and Islam

*Introductory Remarks*: Although *Abraham and His Children* demonstrates how divergent interpretations and traditions sprout from a common root, the video does not address that fact that Muslims and Jews do not read the same account of Abraham in their sacred texts. This section of the program allows the participants to discover for themselves some of the material discussed in Reuven Firestone's article "Abraham: The First Jew or the First Muslim? Text, Tradition, and 'Truth' in Interreligious Dialogue." As Firestone explains, the textual comparison shows that "the Jewish and the Islamic sources of the Abraham-Ishmael legend represent two different, and in many respects contradictory versions of sacred history, each based upon a different sacred scripture." This segment of the program begins with a brief survey of Jewish and Islamic literary traditions in order to orient the participants as to how the texts they will study fit into the larger body of Jewish and Islamic literature.

1. Introduction to Jewish texts:

   a. Briefly explain the Bible, Mishnah, Talmud, and Midrash in terms of chronology, content, and the connections between these works.

   b. Recommended background reading:

      1. Barry W. Holtz, ed., *Back to the Sources* (New York: Summit Books, 1984).

      2. *The Encyclopaedia Judaica*: Related articles.

2. Introduction to Islamic literature:

a. Briefly describe the origin and general content of the Qur'an.

b. Explain the following: *Sunna* (the practice of the Prophet Muhammad, including his deeds, words, and unspoken approval of others), *Hadith* (a record of the sayings of the Prophet), *Shari'a* (Islamic legislation based on the Qur'an and Sunna).

c. Give an overview of the categories of quranic interpretive literature: *Tafsir* (formal exegesis of the Qur'an), *Ta'rikh* (historical works), *Qisas al anbiya* ("Tales of the Prophets," popular hagiographic literature—see section 4b below).

d. Recommended background reading:

1. The *Shorter Encyclopaedia of Islam*, ed. H.A.R. Gibb and J.H. Kramers (Leiden: E.J. Brill, 1991): related articles.

2. Reuven Firestone, "Biblicists and Arabs" and "The Nature of the Literature," in *Journeys in Holy Lands: The Evolution of the Abraham-Ishmael Legends in Islamic Exegesis* (Albany: State University of New York Press, 1990), 3-21.

3. *Hagar and Ishmael in the Hebrew Bible—Cast Out But Not Forgotten*:

a. Distribute the hand-out and read Gen. 21:9-21 and Gen. 25:7-18.

b. What do we learn about Ishmael in these passages?

c. What do we *not* learn about Ishmael in these texts?

1. Point out that Ishmael does not appear in the Genesis narrative in between these two passages. In other words, besides the information given about Ishmael in Gen. 21:20-21 (that he became a bowman and married an Egyptian woman) and in Gen. 25:7-18 (that he returned to bury his father, bore twelve sons, dwelt near Egypt, and lived one hundred and thirty-seven

years), the Hebrew Bible provides only a few details about Ishmael's life.

4. *Hagar and Ishmael in Islamic Literature—From Syria to Mecca*:

   a. Distrubute the hand-out and read Qur'an 14:37.

      1. This passage recounts how Abraham settled Ishmael in an uncultivated valley near Mecca in order to establish regular prayer. In another passage (2:124-129), Abraham and Ishmael are credited with raising the foundations of the *Ka'ba* in Mecca, the ritual center of Islam and the focal point of the *Hajj*.

      2. Note that while several other passages in the Qur'an (such as 3:96-97 and 22:26) refer to Abraham and Ishmael's activities in Mecca, the Qur'an does not explain how they arrived in this holy city. According to Firestone, the Qur'an does not provide this information because "it rather assumes that its audience already knows the answer."

   b. Introduce al-Tabari and his retelling of the Abraham legends:

      1. Muhammad b. Jarir al-Tabari (839-923) is an important Islamic scholar who wrote a commentary on the Qur'an and a history of Islam which spans from Creation to the year 915.

      2. His monumental historical work, *History of Prophets and Kings,* represents the category of Islamic interpretive literature known as *Qisas al-anbiya*, "Tales of the Prophets." In this work, he draws upon oral and literary sources in presenting various versions of Islamic historical events.

      3. For example, in the section under consideration, the legends of Hagar and Ishmael arriving near Mecca, al-Tabari preserves eight slightly different versions of how Hagar, Ishmael, and

Abraham traveled to Mecca and built God's House. The text examined in this program represents one of these eight versions.

4. See Firestone, "Abraham: The First Jew or the First Muslim?" for a discussion of this section of the Abraham story. Also see *The History of al-Tabari*, Vol. 2, *Prophets and Patriarchs*, trans. William M. Brinner (Albany: State University of New York Press, 1987), 69-78; and Firestone, *Journeys in Holy Lands,* 63-71.

c. Read the selection from *The History of Al-Tabari*.

1. After reading the passage, ask a participant to summarize this version of the Hagar and Ishmael story in his or her own words.

2. Point out that in Islamic texts the relationship between Ishmael and Abraham does not end with their arrival in Mecca. Recount Abraham's subsequent three visits to Ishmael (see Firestone, "Abraham").

d. Compare the two stories:

1. How is the Islamic legend similar to the account in Genesis?

2. In what ways are the two traditions different?

## III. Searching for Answers: Approaches to Conflicting Traditions

*Introductory Remarks:* This part of the program explores the question of what we gain by comparing two different scriptural traditions. More importantly, this section addresses the issue of how to explain and live with conflicting religious truth claims.

1. In Program #1, the participants discussed the following statement: "Only by directly confronting our deepest differences can we come to know one another fully. We are who we are as much by our divergence from one another as by our similarity. Paradoxical as it sounds, I do not think we properly comprehend our

own religion until we see it in distinctive difference from other human faiths." [1]

    a. How does studying the Jewish and Islamic versions of the Abraham story support the notion that we better understand one another and ourselves by confronting our differences?

    b. For the Jewish participants: What does learning about the Islamic Abraham legends add to your reading of the Biblical story?

    c. For the Muslim participants: How does reading the Genesis narrative affect your understanding of the Islamic Abraham traditions?

2.    While we may gain much from confronting our differences, we are still left with the difficult question of how to reconcile "two different, and in many respects contradictory versions of sacred history, each based upon a different sacred scripture" (Firestone). In "Abraham: The First Jew or the First Muslim?" Firestone describes several approaches to explain the existence of competing religious beliefs. He writes that "the question of which is the 'original' text is a compelling one but it is, in the end, the wrong question for people desirous of dialogue." [2] Instead, he concludes: "The more productive question is, can we accept the fact that we have different assumptions and beliefs and still live together? In the world of dialogue, the term 'mutual respect' is the key, not 'right' or 'wrong.'"

---

[1] Eugene B. Borowitz, *Contemporary Christologies* (New York: Paulist Press, 1980), 20.

[2] Regarding the origin of and relationship between Jewish and Islamic Abraham narratives, in *Journeys in Holy Lands*, Firestone writes: "The Islamic legends about Abraham are indeed influenced by the Biblicist legends extant in pre-Islamic Arabia and early Islamic society, but they also exhibit influences from indigenous Arabian culture as well as styles, structures, and motifs that are unique to Islam. The legends in Islamic sources are not 'borrowed,' but are rather unique creations fully intelligible only when a prior body of discourse—stories, ideas, legends, religious doctrine, and so forth – is taken into consideration along with contemporary Islamic worldviews" (p. 19).

a. How does reading with "mutual respect" influence our understanding of our sacred texts?

### IV.  Looking Ahead: Preparation for Program #3

1.  In preparation for the Holiday Food Fair in Program #3, ask for volunteers to bring foods associated with the different Jewish and Islamic holidays.  Given the influence of culture and geography, culinary traditions for the different festivals will probably differ among the participants; this variety presents an opportunity to highlight the regional differences in Judaism and Islam.

a. Islamic Holidays: [1]

1.  Id al-Fitr (end of Ramadan)

2.  Suhur (meal eaten before dawn during Ramadan)

3.  Iftar (meal that breaks the fast after sundown during Ramadan)

4.  Id al-Adha (festival of sacrifice celebrated during the  month of the Hajj)

5.  Milad-an-Nabi (the birthday of the Prophet Muhammad)

6.  Muharram (Islamic New Year)

b. Jewish Holidays:

1.  Rosh Hashanah

2.  Sukkot

3.  Hanukkah

---

[1]  The fourth Pillar of Islam ordains the observance of the fast of Ramadam and the celebration of Id al-Fitr.  Id al-Fitr and Id al-Adha are the only two officially recognized Islamic holy days.  The other celebrations are not religious festivals, but celebrations that mark occasions in Islamic history, especially as related to the life of the Prophet Muhammad.

4. Purim

5. Passover

6. Shavuot

2. Discuss the dietary restrictions those preparing food will need to take into consideration.

**Materials:**

1. Copies of the following texts:

   a. *Hagar and Ishmael in the Hebrew Bible: Cast Out But Not Forgotten*

   b. *Abraham, Hagar, Ishmael Through Islamic Eyes: From Syria to Mecca*

2. Name tags

# HAGAR AND ISHMAEL IN THE HEBREW BIBLE: CAST OUT BUT NOT FORGOTTEN

## GENESIS 21:9-15

Sarah saw the son whom Hagar the Egyptian had borne to Abraham playing. She said to Abraham: "Cast out that slave-woman and her son, for the son of that slave shall not share in the inheritance with my son Isaac." The matter distressed Abraham greatly, for it concerned a son of his. But God said to Abraham, "Do not be distressed over the boy or your slave; whatever Sarah tells you, do as she says, for it is through Isaac that offspring shall be continued for you. As for the son of the slave-woman, I will make a nation of him, too, for he is your seed."

Early next morning Abraham took some bread and a skin of water, and gave them to Hagar. He placed them over her shoulder, together with the child, and sent her away. And she wandered about in the wilderness of Beer-sheba. When the water was gone from the skin, she left the child under one of the bushes, and went and sat down at a distance, a bowshot away; for she thought, "Let me not look on as the child dies." And sitting thus afar, she burst into tears.

God heard the cry of the boy, and an angel of God called to Hagar from heaven and said to her, "What troubles you, Hagar? Fear not, for God has heeded the cry of the boy where he is. Come, lift up the boy and hold him by the hand, for I will make a great nation of him." Then God opened her eyes and she saw a well of water. She went and filled the skin with water, and let the boy drink. God was with the boy and he grew up; he dwelt in the wilderness and became a bowman. He lived in the wilderness of Paran; and his mother got a wife for him from the land of Egypt.

## GENESIS 25:7-18

This was the total span of Abraham's life: one hundred and seventy-five years. And Abraham breathed his last, dying at a good ripe age, old and contented; and he was gathered to his kin. His sons Isaac and Ishmael buried him in the cave of Machpelah, in the field of Ephron son of Zohar the Hittite, facing Mamre, the field that Abraham had bought from the Hittites; there Abraham was buried, and Sarah his wife. After the death of Abraham, God blessed his son Isaac. And Isaac settled near Beer-lahai-roi.

This is the line of Ishmael, Abraham's son, whom Hagar the Egyptian, Sarah's slave, bore to Abraham. These are the names of the sons of Ishmael, by their names, in the order of their birth: Nebaioth, the first-born of Ishmael, Kedar, Adbeel, Mibsam, Mishma, Dumah, Massa, Hadad, Tema, Jetur, Naphish, and Kedmah. These are the sons of Ishmael and these are their names by their villages and by their encampments; twelve chieftains of as many tribes. These were the years of the life of Ishmael: one hundred and thirty-seven years; then he breathed his last and died, and was gathered to his kin. They dwelt from Havilah, by Shur, which is close to Egypt, all the way to Asshur; they camped alongside all their kinsmen.

**Source:**

*Tanakh* (Philadelphia: The Jewish Publication Society, 1985), 30 & 37.

# HAGAR AND ISHMAEL IN ISLAMIC LITERATURE: FROM SYRIA TO MECCA

### Qur'an 14:37

O Our Lord! I have made some of my offspring dwell in a valley without cultivation, by Thy Sacred House, in order, O Our Lord, that they may establish regular prayer. So fill the hearts of some people with love towards them, and feed them with fruits so that they may give thanks.

### The History of Al-Tabari

According to Ya'qub b. Ibrahim and al Hasan b. Muhammad—Isma'il b. Ibrahim—Ayyub—Sa'id b. Jubayr—Ibn 'Abbas: The first person to run between al-Safa and al-Marwah was the mother of Ishmael. And the first Arab woman who voided ordure and dragged the edges of her garment over it was the mother of Ishmael. When she fled from Sarah, she let her garment trail behind her to wipe her footprints out. Abraham took her and Ishmael until he reached the place of the House with them, and he left them there. Then he set off to go back to Syria. She followed him and said, "To what have you entrusted us? What will we drink?" At first he did not answer, but then she said: "Did God order you to do this?" He replied, "Yes." She said, "Then He will not let us go astray." So she went back, and Abraham kept going. When he reached a mountain pass full of large rocks and came upon the valley, he said, "My Lord! I have settled some of my posterity in an uncultivable valley near Your Holy House, etc." (Qur'an 14:37).

Hagar had a worn-out waterskin which contained some water, but it gave out and she became thirsty. Then her milk ceased and Ishmael became thirsty. So she looked for the lowest mountain in the area—it was al-Safa—and climbed it. Then she listened, hoping to hear a voice or to see a friendly person. But she did not hear anything, so she climbed down. When she reached the valley she ran even though she did not want to run, as is sometimes the case with exhausted people. Then she looked for another low mountain and climbed la-Marwah to have another look around. Then she heard a faint voice. Being unsure that she had really heard it, she said, "Hush!" to herself, until she was sure of it. Then she said, "You have made me hear Your voice, so give me water, for I am dying and so is the one with me."

The angel took her to the place of Zamzam. Then he stamped his foot, and a spring gushed forth. Hagar hurried to fill her waterskin. The messenger of God said, "May God have mercy on the mother of Ishmael! If she had not been in such a hurry, Zamzam would still be a free-flowing spring." The angel said to her, "Do not fear that the people of this town will go thirsty for this is a spring made for God's guests to drink. The father of this boy will come, and they will build a House on this site."

**Sources:**

*The Meaning of the Holy Qur'an*, 'Abdullah Yusuf Ali (Brentwood, MD: Amana Corporation, 1991). *The History of al-Tabari*, vol. 2, trans. William M. Brinner (Albany: State University of New York Press, 1987), 74-75.

**Program #3**

# HOLIDAYS: A YEAR IN THE LIFE OF MUSLIMS AND JEWS

## Overview:

Both Islam and Judaism follow their own calendars, marking months and years in different ways than our secular calendar. This program explores the Islamic and Jewish holidays celebrated each year. Besides presenting information on the festival calendars in a visual and edible manner, the program is designed to allow the participants to work together and teach one another about their traditions.

## Outline:

I.   The Calendar: Marking Sacred Time

II.  The Holidays: Charting the Year

III. Looking Ahead: Preparation for Program #4

IV.  Holiday Food Fair: A Taste of the Holidays

## Procedure:

### I.   The Calendar: Marking Sacred Time

1. The Islamic Calendar:

   a. Give the month, date, and year according to the Islamic calendar and explain several basic facts:

   1. The Islamic year contains 354 or 355 days and consists of twelve months, each of which begins with the new moon.

2. The counting of the Islamic year began on July 15 or 16, 622 C.E., the first day of the year in which Muhammad travelled from Mecca to Medina (the Hajj).

3. Since Muhammad explicitly abolished the leap year, the new year recedes by ten or eleven days per year. As a result, Islamic festivals are not always celebrated during the same seasons year after year.

2. The Jewish Calendar:

a. Give the month, date, and year according to the Jewish calendar and explain several basic facts:

1. The Jewish calendar is "lunisolar," meaning that the twelve months of the year are marked by the cycle of the moon and the years by the sun.

2. Like the Islamic calendar, each month begins with the new moon (celebrated as *Rosh Chodesh*).

3. The counting of the Hebrew year dates back to the estimated date of the creation of the world.

4. Because many Jewish holidays are tied to the agricultural year and connected in the Bible to specific seasons (Passover, for example, must be celebrated in the spring), it is necessary to adjust the lunar calendar (which contains 354 days per year) to the solar calendar (which contains 365 days per year). Therefore an additional month is added every few years. As a result, unlike the Islamic calendar, the holidays will fall on different dates year after year, but they will always fall in the same season.

## II. The Holidays: Charting the Year

1. Instructions: The Muslim and Jewish participants will work in two separate groups, each with the task of drawing a calendar or creating some other visual presentation outlining their holidays as they occur

during the year.

a. In addition to the yearly holidays, participants should decide how to fit in weekly or daily observances, such as *Salat* (ritual prayer recited five times per day) or Shabbat.

b. One or two members of each group should be prepared to give a brief explanation of the holidays.

1. Divide into groups and distribute materials (paper, pens, calendars).

2. After both groups have finished, come back together and ask a representative from each group to present the project and explain the holidays.

### III. Looking Ahead: Preparation for Program #4

1.  Unlike the holidays, which take place once a year, life cycle events occur throughout the year and throughout our lives.p  The next program will focus on this topic.

2.  Ask for volunteers to prepare presentations on a specific life cycle event.  Each volunteer should (1) briefly explain the customs and background of the ceremony or event and (2) bring photographs of the event or ritual items used during the life cycle celebration.

a. Islamic life cycle events:

1. Naming (Aqikha)

2. Marriage (Nikaah)

3. Death/Mourning (Janaazah)

b, Jewish life cycle events:

1. Naming/Brit Mila/Brit Banot

2. Bar/Bat Mitzvah

3. Marriage

4. Death/Mourning

## IV. Holiday Food Fair: A Taste of the Holidays

1. Ask the participants who brought food to explain the contents and context of the dish, describing the holiday on which it is eaten and any other significant information about the food item.

2. Eat and enjoy!

## Materials:

1. Several large pieces of butcher paper or construction paper

2. Colored marking pens

3. Jewish calendar

4. Islamic calendar

5. Plates, napkins, cups, etc.

6. Name tags

**Program #4**

# LIFE CYCLE: THE RHYTHM OF OUR RELIGIOUS LIVES

## Overview:

This program explores several facets of what it means to be a religious person: the events that mark our growth and the decisions that guide our daily lives. The first part of the program provides an opportunity for the participants to teach each other about their faith's life cycle traditions. The second part asks the participants to discuss how their decisions and daily lives are affected by their religious heritage and ethnic identity.

## Outline:

I.   Life Cycle: Picturing the Lives of Muslims and Jews

II.  Daily Decisions: How Does Who We Are Affect What We Do?

III. Looking Ahead: Preparation for Programs #5 and #6

## Procedure:

### I. Life Cycle: Picturing the Lives of Muslims and Jews

1. The Islamic Life Cycle:

   a. Ask Muslims participants to describe the background and customs of their assigned life cycle event and explain their photograph or ritual item.

2. The Jewish Life Cycle:

   a. Repeat the above process with the Jewish presenters.

## II. Daily Decisions: How Does Who We Are Affect What We Do?

*Introductory Remarks*: This section of the program examines the question of how our religious and ethnic identities affect our decisions and actions. The *Dilemmas & Decisions* activity is intended to point out the diversity of our communities and the complexity of our lives as Muslims and Jews. The discussions will also allow the participants to discover when and how our religious traditions bring us together and set us apart, thereby providing greater insight into our differences and similarities. To a large extent, the success of this activity depends upon the trust, openness, and acceptance that has hopefully developed among the participants by this stage in the dialogue process.

1. Divide the participants into groups of four (two Muslims and two Jews in each group).

2. Give each group a *Dilemmas & Decisions Instruction Sheet* and a set of cards. They should read the instructions and begin the activity.

3. At the conclusion of the activity, bring the small groups together and discuss the following wrap-up questions:

   a. Which issues generated the most agreement between the Muslims and Jews in your group?

   b. Which situations presented the greatest disagreement?

   c. What factors do you think contributed to the differing opinions?

   d. What would you cite as the reasons for the similarities in your responses?

## III. Looking Ahead: Preparation for Programs #5 and #6

1. The next two programs will involve visits to a synagogue and a mosque. In preparation, pass out paper

and pens and ask the participants to write down one or two questions they would like the Rabbi/Imam to answer or general topics they would like addressed during the visits.

**Materials:**

1. Copies of *Dilemmas & Decisions* cards and instruction sheets (one set of cards and one instruction sheet for each group of four)
2. Blank paper
3. Pencils or pens

# DILEMMAS & DECISIONS: INSTRUCTION SHEET

*Dilemmas & Decisions* is a relatively simple activity—all you need to do is read a card and answer a question. While this activity does not demand any technical skills or scholarly knowledge, it does require openness, self-reflection, and imagination.

*Here's how it works:*

1. Beginning with the first card in the stack, select one member of the group to read the dilemma and decision out-loud. The order of the cards does not matter—feel free to select the topics that are most interesting to you.

2. The person who read the card should answer the question and then explain how being a Muslim/Jew influenced his or her decision (see "Things to think about").

3. Give the person of the same faith an opportunity to respond to the situation and explain his or her answer.

4. Ask the other group members to explain how they would answer the question.

*Things to think about:*

1. Can you point to specific religious teachings that shaped your decision?

2. What other factors besides religious values influenced your answer?

3. Have you ever experienced a situation similar to the one described on the card?

# DILEMMAS & DECISIONS:
## How Does Who We Are
## Affect What We Do?

*(Photocopy the following 3 pages in order to make use of the Dilemma & Decision cards)*

✂ ------------------------------------------------------------------------

**DILEMMA:**

A good friend comes to you and asks your advice about the following situation: Your friend is a single mother with a high school aged daughter and a son in junior high school. She earns enough money to support her family by herself and to maintain a modest three bedroom house with two bathrooms, a kitchen, dining room, and living room. Her recently widowed father has suffered a mild stroke and is no longer able to live on his own. While your friend and her father live in the same city, her two siblings (a sister and brother, both of whom are married) live in a different part of the country.

**DECISION:**

Your friend must decide how to respond to this situation. What advice would you give her?

✂ ------------------------------------------------------------------------

**DILEMMA:**

Here's the good news: You have finally received a long-awaited job promotion. But here's the bad news: The promotion will require you to relocate to one of two cities, one with a large Islamic/Jewish population and the other with almost no Muslims/Jews.

**DECISION:**

Your employer will allow you to decide between these two locations. How would this difference influence your decision? To which city would you move?

**DILEMMA:**

It is a week after Thanksgiving, and the stores in your community are already flooded with Christmas decorations and holiday gift items. Your seven year old child has come home from school and asked if your family can buy a Christmas tree and put up lights on the front of your house.

**DECISION:**

What would you tell your child?

✂ --------------------------------------------------------------------------

**DILEMMA:**

You have just received a call informing you that (a) the front of your synagogue has been defaced with swastikas or (b) "Go home Arabs!" has been painted on all sides of your mosque.

**DECISION:**

How would you expect the synagogue/mosque to respond to this situation?

✂ --------------------------------------------------------------------------

**DILEMMA:**

Looking through your mail at the end of the week, you notice that you have received numerous fundraising requests from various charitable organizations. Some of the requests are from Islamic/Jewish causes, others from secular organizations (such as the Cancer Society or the NAACP).

**DECISION:**

Would you send money to any of these causes? If so, how would you decide which organizations to give to and how much money to donate?

**DILEMMA:**

Frustrated by the large class sizes and inadequate equipment in your children's public school classes and worried that they are not learning enough about Islam/Judaism in their supplemental religious education, you are contemplating sending your children to the Islamic/Jewish school in your neighborhood.

**DECISION:**

List the pros and cons of an Islamic/Jewish school education. If the cost of private school was not an issue, would you send your children to an Islamic/Jewish school? Why or why not?

------------------------------------------------------------------------

**DILEMMA:**

You have just found out that an extremely important business meeting has been scheduled on the same day as Rosh Hashanah/Id al-Fitr.

**DECISION:**

How would you respond to this situation?

------------------------------------------------------------------------

**DILEMMA:**

Your twenty-one year old son has called you from his college and informed you that while taking a Comparative Religions class, he met a non-Muslim/non-Jewish woman whom he has been dating seriously for eight months.

**DECISION:**

What would you tell your son? Would your response differ if the scenario involved a daughter?

**Programs #5 & #6**

# SYNAGOGUE AND MOSQUE VISITS: ENTERING THE WORLD OF PRAYER

**Overview:**

This phase of the dialogue is intended to introduce the participants to the mosque and the synagogue. In addition to teaching about Jewish and Islamic prayer, the visits present an opportunity to learn about the other activities held in the synagogue/mosque and to address the broader question of how the synagogue/mosque fits into the life of the larger Jewish/Islamic community. [1] The structure and precise content of the visits has been left to the determination of the Rabbi and the Imam. Provided below is a list of suggested topics and activities. These ideas, along with the questions compiled at the end of Program #4, should serve as a guide for planning the visit.

**Suggested Topics and Activities:**

**I.  Islamic and Jewish Worship**

1.  Explain the components of the worship service.

    a. Hand-out prayerbooks or other items used during the service.

    b. Outline the times in which worship takes place.

---

[1]  For an excellent discussion of "The Mosque: Its Form, Constituency, and Function" and "The Imam," see Yvonne Yazbeck Haddad and Adair T. Lummis, *Islamic Values in the United States*, 24-66.

c. Give a brief overview of the content of the liturgy and the formation of the prayerbook.

d. Talk about the usage of Arabic/Hebrew in the service.

2. Discuss the role of the Rabbi/Imam in the service.

a. How do other worshipers participate in the service?

b. Do men and women have different roles in the worship service? Explain.

3. Address the place of music in the service and in other Jewish/Islamic ceremonies.

a. Arrange for a demonstration of Jewish/Islamic music.

4. Explain the history and significance of the physical space in which prayer takes place.

## II. The Role of the Mosque or Synagogue in the Life of the Community

1. Tour the facility.

2. Describe the activities held in the synagogue/mosque.

a. Hand out a calendar or newsletter that list the upcoming events.

3. Explain the educational system of the mosque/synagogue.

a. Display a sampling of the text books used in the school or in other educational activities.

4. Outline the responsibilities of the professional staff.

a. If available, introduce the staff. Ask them to explain their responsibilities and discuss how they contribute to the life of the mosque/synagogue.

b. Explain the training required for an Imam/Rabbi.

c. Describe a typical day for the Imam/Rabbi.

5. Describe the leadership and organizational structure of the synagogue/mosque.

a. Ask a board member to greet the group.

b. Arrange for one of the groups within the synagogue/mosque to prepare a reception for the group.

6.  Discuss how the synagogue/mosque fits into the larger Jewish/Islamic community.

    a. Approximately what percentage of Muslims/Jews affiliate with a mosque/synagogue?

    b. Besides or in addition to joining a mosque/synagogue, to what other Islamic/Jewish organizations might people belong?

    c. If you were trying to convince someone to join your synagogue/mosque, what would you tell them? Describe what you see as the most important reasons for being involved in a synagogue/mosque.

## Looking Ahead: Preparation for Program #7:

1.  Because much of Jewish/Islamic life take place not in the synagogue/mosque, but in the home, it is fitting to follow these two sessions with home visits.

2.  At the end of Program #6, ask for a list of volunteers who would like to welcome several participants to their homes for a meal (dinner or dessert) and discussion (the hosts will also lead the discussion).

3.  Determine who will host whom or make the arrangements afterwards and notify the participants over the phone or through the mail.

4.  Ask the participants to read "Philosophical Developments in Islam and Judaism: A Medieval Model for Philosophical Development" by Leonard Kravitz and "Judeo-Arab Fraternity Rediscovered" by Abdelwahab Hechiche.

5.  Hand out *Discussion Guidelines* to the hosts and remind them of any dietary restrictions that should be taken into consideration.

**Looking Ahead: Preparation for Program #8:**

1.  If the facilitators would like to involve participants in planning the closing ritual, ask for volunteers and set a meeting time (see Program #8).

**Materials (for Program #6):**

1.  Copies of the *Discussion Guidelines* for the hosts.

**Program #7**

# HOME HOSPITALITY: CONFRONTING OUR PAST AND BUILDING OUR FUTURE

## Overview:

The format and content of this program reflect several goals. First, by bringing small groups together in each other's homes, the participants will hopefully strengthen the bonds of friendship that have been forming over the previous six programs. Because this format presents a less structured, more social setting, participants will have an opportunity for open discussion and personal sharing. Second, such an environment provides a good chance to reflect upon the history of our two communities. This segment of the program looks back at the historical relationships between Muslims and Jews and questions how our understanding of the past influences our potential for the future.

## Outline:

I.   Dinner or Dessert

II.  Story: The Two-Sided Dual

III. Discussion: Interpreting Our Past

# CONFRONTING OUR PAST AND BUILDING OUR FUTURE: *A DISCUSSION GUIDE*

## A Few Notes to the Host:

- First, thank you for opening up your home and putting in the time and energy spent preparing for this evening.

- Second, besides arranging the meal, serving as a host gives you the additional responsibility of leading a short discussion (approximately 30 minutes). If you have any questions about this material, contact your facilitator.

## Introductory Remarks:

Although our Muslim and Jewish ancestors most likely did not gather in each other's homes for dinner or dessert, they were not complete strangers. Depending on the time and place, Jews and Muslims have co-existed with varying degrees of interaction throughout the centuries. This discussion will examine the past relationship between our two peoples.

The discussion begins with a story that shows how two people can interpret the same event in two different ways. Similarly, the history of the relationship between Muslims and Jews can also be cast in different lights. For example, one person might argue that Jews in Muslim-controlled lands have long been subject to persecution and precariousness; another person might survey the same historical time-frame and conclude that Muslims and Jews have generally coexisted in tolerance and even friendship. Much depends on the evidence we emphasize or the lens through which we look at the past.

Reconstructing history requires us to sift through large quantities of data and numerous, often opposing visions of what happened when. As a result, we must make choices about what to read and who to believe. This process means that in spite of the most valiant attempts at neutrality, our individual perspectives and agendas will influence which events we highlight or ignore and, consequently, what we conclude and what we teach.

This discussion will ask the participants to reflect on their sense of Jewish-Muslim relations past and present.

**Discussion:**

1.  After the meal, or at any other appropriate time in the evening, begin the discussion with a brief introduction and overview.

2.  Ask someone to read "The Two-Sided Dual."

    a. Explain the connection between the story and the topic under discussion.

3.  Suggested questions:

    a. How would you characterize the historical relationship between Muslims and Jews? Select a short phrase or an appropriate metaphor which expresses your understanding of the Muslim-Jewish relationship.

    b. Imagining a spectrum between "Bitter Enemies" and "Close Friends," where would you place Jews and Muslims: (1) In the Middle Ages? (2) Today? (3) Twenty years from now?

    c. How does our attempt to understand our history influence our contemporary relationship?

# THE TWO-SIDED DUAL

One day, the ruler of a small medieval town announced that all of those who had not lived in the town for two consecutive generations would immediately have to pack up and leave. Shocked and distressed by this news, those affected by the decree rushed toward the town square and begged the ruler to allow them to stay. Somewhat swayed by their pleas, the ruler announced that he would rescind the decree if someone could defeat the bishop in a public, non-verbal duel of wits.

Daunted by the ruler's challenge, the townspeople nervously looked around, waiting for someone to volunteer. Finally, a young seamstress stepped forward.

On the day of the competition, the bishop and the seamstress solemnly walked toward the center of the town square. Nodding their heads to acknowledge that the duel had begun, the bishop then drew a large circle on the ground. The seamstress furiously stomped her feet. The bishop looked a bit uneasy, but he continued by holding up three fingers. The seamstress looked at his hand, thought for a few minutes, and then held up one finger. The bishop looked increasingly more nervous. At this point, he took bread and wine from under his garments and held them in his hands for all to see. In response, the seamstress took an apple from her skirt pocket and bit into it. Watching her eat, the bishop shook his head, threw his hands into the air, and shouted: "That's it! You win."

The ruler marched to the center of the town square and announced that no one would be forced to leave. As the townspeople breathed a heavy sigh of relief, he declared: "May you live in this town for generation after generation to come!"

Later that afternoon, the bishop's disciples asked what had happened during the non-verbal duel of wits. He answered: "I drew a circle to remind us that God is everywhere, but the seamstress stomped on the ground to remind me that God is not in Hell. I then held up t' ree fingers to remind us of the Trinity, but she held up one finger to remind me of the oneness of God. Finally, I took out bread and wine, a symbol of the sacrifice of our Lord, but she took out an apple—a reminder of the sin that made salvation necessary."

Across town, a group of friends gathered around the seamstress and asked her how in the world she had defeated the bishop. "Well, he drew a big circle to show that the ruler wanted us outside the city walls, but I stomped on the ground to show that we did not want to leave. He then help up three fingers to announce that the ruler demanded that we move out three days, but I held up one finger to let him know that not one of us would leave. And finally, he took out his lunch, so I took out mine."

## Program #8

# CONCLUSION:
# TOWARD FUTURE JOURNEYS

**Overview:**

This program asks the participants to look both backward and forward, reflecting on what they have gained from the experience of Jewish-Muslim dialogue and projecting where they would like this process to lead. The program returns to a metaphor used in the first program, that of dialogue as a journey.

**Outline:**

I.   Looking Back: Where Has The Journey Taken Us?

II.   Looking Ahead: Where Will The Journey Lead?

III.   Closing Ritual

**Procedure:**

**I.   Looking Back: Where Has The Journey Taken Us?**

1.   Pass out paper and pens/pencils and ask the participants to list the three most important things they have gained or learned in the past seven sessions.

2.   Share the lists.

**II.   Looking Ahead: Where Will The Journey Lead?**

1.   Divide the participants into small groups, giving butcher paper/construction paper and markers to each group. Their task is to write a list of suggestions as to where they would like to see the dialogue

lead. Their proposal should address three potential areas for future activities: (1) the dialogue group, (2) the synagogue/mosque, (3) the larger community.

2. When the groups are finished, ask a representative from each group to present the proposal.

### III. Closing Ritual

1. This segment of the program has been left open in order to allow each dialogue group to create a closing ritual that reflects the personality and experience of the group. As noted at the end of Programs #5 and #6, the facilitators may want to involve participants in planning the ritual.

2. Ideas:

   a. Incorporate the prayers for a journey recited in the first program.

   b. Write a prayer which Muslims and Jews can recite together.

   c. Select a piece of music the participants can all sing (a *niggun*, for example).

   d. Read an appropriate passage from the Bible and the Qur'an.

### Materials:

1. Note-sized pieces of paper
2. Butcher paper or construction paper
3. Colored marking pens
4. Pens or pencils

# BIBLIOGRAPHY

Denny, Frederick M. *Islam*. San Francisco: Harper and Row Publishers, 1987. This book gives a basic introduction to Islamic traditions and the worldwide Muslim community.

Firestone, Reuven. *Journeys in Holy Lands: The Evolution of the Abraham-Ishmael Legends in Islamic Exegesis*. Albany: State University of New York Press, 1990. This work surveys a range of Islamic legends about Abraham from the Qur'an and early Islamic exegesis. These legends are also examined in relation to Jewish, Christian, and pre-Islamic Arabian legends.

Haddad, Yvonne Yazbeck, ed. *The Muslims of America*. New York: Oxford University Press, 1991. This book brings together essays by leading Muslim scholars on the history, challenges, and responses of the Muslim community of U.S. and Canada.

Haddad, Yvonne Yazbeck and Adair T. Lummis. *Islamic Values in the United States*. New York: Oxford University Press, 1987. This sociological study of Muslim immigrants to America and their descendants provides a wealth of information and insight about the Islamic community in America.

Kertzer, Morris N. *What is a Jew?* Revised by Lawrence A. Hoffman. New York: Macmilliam, 1993. This recently revised work provides an excellent introduction to Jewish thought and Jewish life.

Lewis, Bernard. *The Jews of Islam*. Princeton: Princeton University Press, 1984. The author has "tried to examine the origins, the flowering, and the ending of the Jewish-Islamic tradition, and to set these processes against the background of both Jewish and Islamic learning" (xi).

Strassfeld, Michael. *The Jewish Holidays: A Guide and Commentary*. New York: Harper and Row, Publishers, 1985. This book supplements a thorough examination of the history and customs of the Jewish holidays with comments by contemporary scholars.

Stillman, Norman A. *The Jews of Arab Lands: A History and Source Book*. Philadelphia: The Jewish Publication Society, 1979. Through historical analysis and primary source documents, this book explores the Jewish communities in the Islamic world from the time of Muhammad until the nineteenth century.

Syme, Daniel B. *The Jewish Home: A Guide for Jewish Living*. New York: UAHC Press, 1988. This work is an accessible yet thorough explanation of the rituals and practices of holidays, lifecycle, and home celebrations.